Saint Paul
at the Movies

Also by Robert Jewett

Jesus Against the Rapture:
Seven Unexpected Prophecies

Saint Paul
at the Movies

*The Apostle's Dialogue
with American Culture*

Robert Jewett

Westminster/John Knox Press
Louisville, Kentucky

Scripture translations throughout this book are the author's own, unless otherwise indicated.

Scripture quotations marked RSV are from the Revised Standard Version of the Bible, copyright 1946, 1952, © 1971, 1973 by the Division of Christian Education of the National Council of the Churches of Christ in the U.S.A., and are used by permission.

Chapter 5 is a slightly revised and expanded version of Chapter 1, "'Life to the Dead' from the God of Tender Mercies" in *Life as Liberty, Life as Trust,* edited by J. Robert Nelson, copyright 1992 by Wm. B. Eerdmans Publishing Co. Used by permission.

Permission to use material in chapter 3 has been granted by Pickwick Publications for "Sin and Salvation: *Amadeus* in the Light of Romans," in *Ex Auditu: An International Journal of Theological Interpretation of Scripture* 5 (1989), 159–169.

Book design by Drew Stevens

First edition

This book is printed on acid-free paper that meets the American National Standards Institute Z39.48 standard. ⊚

Published by Westminster/John Knox Press
Louisville, Kentucky

PRINTED IN THE UNITED STATES OF AMERICA
9 8 7 6 5 4 3 2 1

Library of Congress Cataloging-in-Publication Data

Jewett, Robert.
    Saint Paul at the movies / Robert Jewett. — 1st ed.
        p.   cm.
    Includes index.
    ISBN 0–664–25482–9 (pbk. : alk. paper)

    1. Bible. N.T. Epistles of Paul—Theology.   2. Motion pictures—Religious aspects—Christianity.   I. Title.
BS2652.J48 1993
225.9'2—dc20   93–1315

Contents

Preface

This book arises from a long-standing interest in relating critical biblical study to the American cultural setting. My colleagues and students at Garrett-Evangelical Theological Seminary have heard preliminary forms of most of these chapters; their encouragement has been invaluable.

The task of relating biblical materials to contemporary films is daunting even with the aid of colleagues, friends, and family members, but without them this project could never have come to fruition. I am especially indebted to the readers of earlier drafts of this project who helped me separate some wheat from much chaff: Patrick H. Alexander, James B. Ashbrook, Phyllis Beattie, Roger Bourland, William Doran, Gerald E. Forshey, Rosemary Skinner Keller, Lallene Rector, and Dean Lanning. Important refinements were suggested by Dennis E. Groh, Ellen Jewett, Jeffrey Mahan, R. Franklin Terry, Mariam Thalos, and Robert Richardson. Decisive critical aid was given by David Rhoads and the members of the class we taught in the fall of 1992, "Biblical Interpretation and Contemporary Film." Participants in the Society of Biblical Literature section, "The Bible in Ancient and Modern Media," including Thomas E. Boomershine, David Rhoads, and Bernard Brandon Scott, have offered significant encouragement as well as theoretical resources over

1

the past decade. Other New Testament scholars in the Association of Chicago Theological Schools have also provided encouragement and critical suggestions.

Movies are the most thoroughly collaborative products of contemporary culture. It is therefore appropriate that this book is indebted to so many partners. There is insufficient space here to name everyone whose insights have influenced this project, including scholars and students, ministers and laypersons, film devotees and cultural critics. Some of their writings are acknowledged in the notes. In the hope that it will encourage others to reflect on the relation between the Bible and the movies, I dedicate this book to the churches, classes, and circles of friends that have already joined the dialogue.

1

Prologue: Pauline Theology Takes In the Movies

For though I am free with respect to all,
    I have made myself a slave to all,
        so that I might win more of them.
To the Jews I became as a Jew,
    in order to win Jews. . . .
To the weak I became weak,
    so that I might win the weak.
I have become all things to all people,
    that I might by all means save some.[1]

                                    (1 Cor. 9:19–22)

Also, do not be conformed to this world,
    but be transformed by the renewal of the mind,
that you may ascertain what is the will of God
    —the good and acceptable and perfect.

                                    (Rom. 12:2)

The apostle Paul would have wanted to extend his journeys into the regions depicted by the movies, had they been available in his time. This Christian theologian, who had been a Jewish theologian before his conversion, struggled throughout his career to bridge the gaps between regions and cultures. In the famous passage quoted above concerning his desire to accommodate himself to different groups, Paul touches on some of the barriers that divided the ancient society. Jews did not ordinarily associate with non-Jews, nor the socially strong with the weak. Greco-Roman society was splintered and class bound, obsessed with status, and inclined to intense levels of competition between persons and groups. The church in Corinth was split into competitive factions. Yet Paul's gospel was that Christ had died for all, and that all must therefore be reconciled. His efforts to get on the wavelengths of these factions led to the charge that he was too wishy-washy,[2] which provoked him to set forth the rationale of a free person becoming "a slave to all."

Although this inclusive message does not fit with the usual appraisal of Paul as a doctrinaire chauvinist, it would be highly appealing to many today. But should being "all things to all people" really include taking in the movies? They are secular forms of entertainment, produced for profit, conveying cultural ideals and norms that are often far from those of religious communities. And in the minds of many highly trained scholars, oriented more to books than to films, there is a cultural abyss between the realms of theological analysis and historical research on the one hand and popular culture on the other. It is acceptable to employ advanced hermeneutical or communicative theories to explain Paul's thought, because these theories come from the same sophisticated level as the tradition of Pauline theology. But popular movies function in the arena of the general public and seem to require no great sophistication for their understanding. Self-respecting scholars are understandably reluctant to become "weak" in order to "win the weak." Whatever the reasons, few biblical studies have taken insights from contemporary cinema into account.

Reasons to Take In the Movies

This book makes a case that Pauline theology in the American scene should now begin to take account of the movies. One reason is that many contemporary Americans are shaped much more decisively by popular culture than by their formal education or their religious training. Paul's method was to place himself where other people were, to communicate the gospel on their turf. In our day, that clearly should involve the movies, which are a primary arena for discovering and debating important moral, cultural, and religious issues. If we wish to follow Paul's cue, becoming an observant Jew in order to communicate with Jews or a freedom-loving Greek to communicate with the Greeks, it is essential that ministers, teachers, and laypersons interested in the impact of the faith should begin to take more seriously the growing cultural force of the movies and videos. Attendance in movie theaters is currently twenty million per week, much lower than the ninety-five million per week in 1929. But far more movies are seen on home video systems than in theaters, now that more than 80 percent of American households have video equipment. Rental of movies for home video sets averaged eighty million per week in 1992, while six to seven million videos are purchased each week. Films and videos occupy a large portion of the time and attention of the youth culture in particular, becoming a decisive element in shaping the identity of the next generation.[3] The potential of Paul's thought for creative interaction with American culture will remain untapped if it does not take account of these formative materials in popular culture.

Another reason Pauline theology should take in the movies has to do with the recent discovery of the primary locale of his missionary work. Recent scholarship has shown that the workshop rather than the synagogue, lecture hall, or street corner was the place where indirect evangelism took place.[4] Paul spent long days in the secular arena of a tentmaking shop, conversing with customers, neighbors, and visitors. The workshop in the ancient world was similar to the barbershop or beauty shop in more recent American experience, a place where extended conversations could

5

take place. There are numerous references to philosophical and current issues being discussed in such a setting. Workshops were in the marketplace near the theaters and temples and forums of Greco-Roman cities. A similar case could be made for the likely location of many early Christian churches, using the living spaces and workshops of the inner city. There were no church buildings or rooms dedicated exclusively to church use until centuries later. The arena of Pauline Christianity was secular rather than sacred. The comparable location in contemporary society would probably be the living room or coffee shop where recent films and videos are being watched and discussed.

I believe Paul would have been a discerning partner in discussing secular movies, had they been available in his time. The issues they raise and the stories they tell would have been reminiscent of conversations in the workshops where he spent most of his life. In fact, in the light of what we now know, the purely religious and academic arenas in which Paul has been discussed in Western culture may have seriously distorted the scope and implications of his theology. I hope in this book to make a modest step toward reconnecting Paul with the kind of social and cultural context in which his contribution may be more fully recognized.

This study is part of a larger effort on my part to relate Paul's theology to contemporary American culture.[5] A companion to this study of Paul and the movies, dealing with developments in Pauline research that have been decisively influenced by American cultural trends, will be published in 1994.[6] This work emerges from a growing awareness that Pauline theology has been bound too long to its Eurocentric origins. This area of biblical study has remained almost entirely within the parameters defined by the European Reformation and the resultant conflicts between Protestants, Catholics, and Jews. This has resulted in significant distortions of certain aspects of his thought and a weakened capacity to relate his contribution to the American cultural setting. In contrast to other areas of biblical study, a fully indigenized view of Paul's theology has not yet been developed in this country. I think we have failed to carry through with Paul's program to function as "a Greek to the Greeks, a Jew to the Jews . . . and an American to the Americans." In this book I want to free Pauline theology from the burdens of its traditional, Eurocentric formulation and to relate its transforming potential to the American cultural situation.

The Interpretive Approach

The studies that I have seen on the topic of religion and film do not take biblical theology into account, much less the potential contribution of the Pauline letters.[7] But they provide a stimulus for my approach in this book. Some of these studies use films as illustrations of established doctrines.[8] I would prefer to approach films on the assumption that they disclose truth in their own right and thus qualify as valid conversation partners in dialogue with Pauline letters. A serious encounter with movies allows contextual forms of truth to emerge from the dialogue itself. This approach would be consistent with that of the essayists in the volume titled *Religion in Film,* who avoid reading "religious meaning *into* films" and seek "to discover the harmony of the *whole* in terms of the language of film itself,"[9] even though none of them displays an interest in dialogue with biblical materials.

I appreciate the religious film critics who urge respect for the integrity of films, but I prefer an approach that might be called "dialogue in a prophetic mode." I want to deal with a film in tandem with a specific biblical passage, treating both with equal respect, and bringing their themes and metaphors into relationship so that a contemporary interpretation for the American cultural situation may emerge. If films are visual stories with parabolic quality, they can be related to the biblical stories that contemporary scholarship has reconstructed with regard to each of the Pauline letters. Behind each Pauline letter there is a lively community in the early church, with its particular crisis and resolution, so that the text comprises a decisive part of a larger story. I am not as much interested in evaluating films on the basis of aesthetic criteria as in discerning the message these interacting "stories" disclose for our society. And although I grant precedence to the biblical text, I am committed to the principle that the truth must always be prophetically discerned within a particular context at a particular time. So I am not inclined to criticize films because of their disparity with traditional doctrines. My task in this book is not film criticism, for which I have neither the talent nor the training, but rather culturally contextual interpretation.

An outstanding example of film criticism from a religious point of view is available in Richard A. Blake's *Screening America*,[10] the usefulness of which at this point is to develop the contours of my approach. Like John R. May and his colleagues in *Religion in Film*, Blake emphasizes the autonomy of movies "that must not and cannot be baptized and then coerced into ecclesial servitude."[11] Blake takes account of cinematic predecessors and broad cultural concerns. I particularly appreciate his effort to use the history of film to provide access to American culture. I admire his apt way of allowing films to speak for themselves, without the imposition of inappropriate theological or moralistic systems. But there is little sense of the prophetic power of the message either of these films or of the theological themes he detects. The potentially vivid counterweight of biblical stories and ideas is not allowed to come into the picture.

What I would like to do is emulate Blake's respect for the autonomy of the film while initiating a dialogue with another story, drawn from Pauline letters. Although I cannot command the mastery of cinematic history and theory that a professional film critic like Blake displays, I want to concentrate on the connections with the biblical tradition. My hope is that a respectful dialogue that is sensitive to the contemporary relevance of both the film and the biblical text may succeed in throwing new light on the situation faced by individuals and by American culture as a whole. It is the gospel that calls me to respect the contours both of the films and of the biblical texts. I do not find this inconsistent with a commitment to pursue the saving power of the gospel, that it "might by all means save some" (1 Cor. 9:22). As we shall see, when Paul refers to the "gospel," it is anything but the doctrinaire litany of beliefs that is often assumed.

My approach to the relationship between films and biblical texts follows the idea of an interpretive arch, which operates by seeking analogies between ancient and modern texts and situations. I visualize an arch with one end anchored in the ancient world and the other in a contemporary cultural situation. There is a conversation at each end of the arch because the original message was in response to an original situation in the life of the early church. I therefore understand a Pauline text in the light of its bearing on a specific cultural and historical context, and I look for modern analogies not just to the words Paul wrote but also to the situations he addressed. I understand Paul's letters as rhetorically sophisticated efforts to persuade, written for specific rhetorical situations in the life of early Christian communities. An understanding of the words Paul wrote thus depends on understanding the situation and the communities they address. Pauline texts also involve conversations in that his ideas were influenced by his colleagues and were intended to be conveyed and were interpreted by trusted letter bearers; they employ shared communal resources like hymns, confessions, lists of quotations, benedictions, doctrinal traditions, and so forth, drawn from the common life of early Christian congregations. Despite the tradition of abstract, dogmatic interpretation that has tended to dominate Pauline studies, I am operating on the assumption that every word of a Pauline letter is embedded in a story of a concrete community in conversation with other faith communities.

The arch between the ancient moment and the present encompasses the history of interpretation, including some

9

of the greatest theologians in Christendom as well as the Pauline scholars of the past who reinterpreted Paul for their own cultural and historical situations. Each current interpreter's arch contains certain patron saints that shape the contours of his or her particular interpretive tradition. Mine includes Augustine, Luther, Calvin, Wesley, Barth, Ernst Käsemann, and James Dunn among others too numerous to mention. The interpretive arch also contains the popular preachers and teachers of my own particular denominational tradition as well as those who shaped the broader cultural tradition in the United States of America. We each stand in a "community of interpreters."[12] My work with both the Pauline texts and contemporary films is influenced by communities of interpretation inside and outside of the academic realm. No interpreter works alone; we all negotiate the interpretive arch along cables woven by our traditions and our communities.

The contemporary end of the interpretive arch rests in my own denominational and cultural situation, which is why I avoid generalizations that claim to be universal in their scope. My interest is in relating Paul to my own cultural situation. I want to counter the tradition of claiming objectivity in Pauline theology while at the same time avoiding the tendency to think of Paul as an abstract thinker. Since every Pauline letter is embedded in a story, I look for parallel stories in the contemporary world that resonate with the stories behind each letter. In selecting a film to relate to a particular text, I look for thematic and narrative similarities. Once a film is selected, it deserves and requires interpretive efforts equal to those expended on the biblical text itself. Even an amateur like myself can view a film repeatedly, study its structure and dialogue, discuss it with colleagues and friends, and read reviews and articles that relate to its story and meaning. I try to devote the same energy to film exegesis as to biblical text exegesis, although of course my professional training was strictly in the latter. By allowing these stories to interact, the biblical and the cinematic, new insights emerge. I look for the spark that flies between the two arches of the biblical text and the contemporary film. It is a prophetic process in which contextual truths are disclosed that throw light on contemporary situations, both within my faith community and within my civic community and its broader ecumenical horizon. And like all prophetic insights within the Pauline traditions, they bear on particular moments and communities and they are a matter of "prophesying in part," of "seeing through a glass darkly" (1 Cor. 13:8, 12). Whether these sparks light up the present hour must be left for my readers to discern and weigh.

The discipline of the interpretive arch has led me to abandon the tradition of using modern materials as mere "illustrations" of Pauline truth. To illustrate presumes that truth is already fully understood by the speaker, whereas in reality truth is itself dialectical, revealing itself to us in particular historical contexts. Thus I have chosen to interweave Pauline texts with modern stories and issues, allowing each side to throw light on the other. When I select an important novel or film whose themes and story correlate closely with a biblical text, the modern artifact should be treated with a level of respect that allows it to become a full partner in conversation with Paul the apostle. The movie must be seen and interpreted within its cultural context, if our task is to be accomplished. So these essays offer a conversation between several partners, interwoven into what I hope is a coherent whole. But my impulse is prophetic rather than didactic; the creation of holistic vision does not constitute the claim of seeing timeless truth.

I need to make clear, therefore, that while each movie is treated with respect, the Pauline word is allowed to stand as primus inter pares. It is the first among equals because the inspired text of scripture has stood the test of time by revealing ultimate truth that has gripped past and current generations with compelling power when concretized in relation to particular historical circumstances. There are ways in which great movies are also inspired. But biblical texts have sustained the life and morals of faith communities in circumstances both adverse and happy over several thousand years; they are formative in my own denominational community of interpreters as well as in American culture, providing the narrative framework for many forms of contemporary entertainment, not to speak of their effect on the national consciousness and the civil religion. I come from a Wesleyan tradition that wanted to be a religion "of one book," and from a cultural tradition that viewed the Bible as the most decisive book in the world. But although the texts in the Bible deserve to be granted a measure of priority, we shall not find them to be overbearing partners in the dialogue with contemporary films. Like Paul in his willingness to accommodate himself to the needs of various cultural groups, I find that biblical texts when understood in the context of their original stories are flexible, adaptable, and provocative.

On the assumption that Paul was serious when he said he was obligated both to the weak and the strong (1 Corinthians 9), "both to Greeks and barbarians, both to the wise and the uneducated" (Rom. 1:14), I think there is justification for undertaking this adventure in culture dialectics, uniting high culture with low, the sophisticated with the barbaric. We shall consider juxtapositions that may strike many readers as ludicrous, linking the movie *Tootsie* with the exposition of the "comfort of Christ" in 2 Corinthians, or *Star Wars* with the abstract thesis of Romans. If Paul is to function as a fully indigenized apostle to America, it must be the America of low culture as well as high, the barbaric as well as the elite. If he refused to make devious discriminations, his followers should do no less.

Criteria in Interpreting Movies

Paul's generosity in including outsiders did not cripple his capacity to evaluate alternatives. In the ethical admonition of Romans 12, printed at the head of this chapter, the response of faith to the gift of a transformed life is described in terms of communal nonconformity with the world and a constant renewal of the mind. These themes have decisive importance as groups interact with the world of contemporary film. Paul's admonition, "do not be conformed to this world," pertained to the social and political pressure that were part of everyday experience for early Christians. Prior to receiving this letter, the Roman Christians had undergone a period of governmental harassment, as places of Christian and Jewish worship were closed under the Edict of Claudius. It is significant that the admonition not to conform is expressed to the community rather than to the individual. Paul's assumption is that the primary arena of Christian evaluation, decision making, and resistance to an evil environment was the small faith community.

There is a significant resource at this point for groups that are engaged in reflecting on the relation between films and biblical texts in the current situation of national troubles. The logical contemporary locale for such activity is the small group that meets formally or informally to discuss films and texts in the light of faith. While these chapters are written by a single person, they arise out of repeated discussions with congregations and small groups. And the best way to follow up on the impulses of this book is to engage in such dialogue with friends and church members. Such conversations need constantly to be marked by nonconformity with the pressures of the society, whether in the form of widely popular entertainments or seemingly authoritative interpretations. Paul's approach can fill the need for critical interaction and the need to allow both the ancient and modern texts to speak without cultural censorship, whether direct or indirect.

Paul's admonition to "be transformed by the renewal of the mind" is also directed to groups rather than merely to individuals. It relates to the restoration of the original rationality of the human race that was distorted by the Fall

(Rom. 1:18–32), a theme to be discussed in chapters 3 and 4. The element of "newness" is particularly prominent here, the Greek term having been apparently coined by Paul for this occasion. It is related to the newness of life referred to in Romans 6:4 and 7:6. Paul has in mind the recovery of righteousness and rationality through conversion and the ongoing renewal of orientation, since the members of early Christian churches would have consisted of persons converted by the gospel. The contemporary equivalent would be a church group or a circle of Christian friends that discusses films in the light of a shared experience of the New Creation. The wording of Paul's admonition also carries the implication of an ongoing revelation to the community. The "renewed mind" of the Christian community is constantly honed by communal interaction in a process sustained by the Spirit. Such a group consciousness is capable of interacting in fresh and responsible ways with the new creations of our culture, including of course the movies.

Paul goes on to urge that "you [plural] may ascertain what is the will of God—the good and acceptable and perfect," which refers to communal discernment of what God desires in emerging situations. The premise here is that God's will is not static; it must be ascertained from moment to moment, decade to decade, generation to generation. According to Paul this occurs through discussion and shared experiences. Discernment is a rational process, dependent on public debate and mutual criticism.

Paul uses three of the key ethical concepts in the Greco-Roman world to identify the concepts the community may use to make proper assessments. He refers to Christian groups ascertaining the "good and acceptable and perfect." All three categories for moral and intellectual discernment are useful in the discussion of films; their use by film critics is why I have employed such materials in interpreting individual films. These same categories would be useful for any small group as it grapples with these issues, because advocates of each category are likely to be within the group itself.

The "good" referred to in Romans 12:2 refers to the highest moral quality of ancient and modern culture. Although defined in a variety of ways, it was thought to have an abiding quality that transcended specific situations. For Paul it was rooted finally in the nature of God as the source of righteousness. Persons who evaluate films on the basis of absolute, moral, and spiritual values are operating on the basis of this concept.

The "acceptable" is the standard of public ethics and popular choice, relating to local standards and moral sensitivities. This is rather close to what contemporary Americans have in mind in the discussion of "values." They are the values that certain people in certain cultural situations hold to be good, but it is assumed that other groups may differ. Persons who are concerned about public taste and local standards are using contemporary forms of the "acceptable."

The "perfect" alludes to the mystical, aesthetic, philosophical, or religious realms; it includes the arena of "inspiration," which surfaces in the greatest artistic and intellectual creations. People cannot finally measure or define such creations, but they may acknowledge their presence and are drawn by their power. Participants in film discussions who are sensitive to artistic values are probably operating out of the realm of this concept in one form or another.

What I find noteworthy about Paul's ethical stance is that he allows all three categories to stand alongside one another while suggesting that each requires ongoing discernment by the community. Even the "good" and the "perfect" must be examined and evaluated, which was a stunning claim for any ancient writer to make. Paul's idea is that the renewed mind of the Christian community, as well as the embodiment of the "mercies of God" (Rom. 12:1) conveyed to the human race in the Christ event provide the guidelines by which all products of culture are to be evaluated.

Given their ubiquity and power, the movies are among the most prominent targets for this process of moral and spiritual discernment in our society. But the process requires the insights of the whole community and should not be relegated entirely to the work of specialists and critics. The same must be said of this book and of the reviews of films. They may provide significant resources for discussion, but they can go only part way along the path of ascertaining what is the will of God for any particular moment, for a particular group of people. Such discernment is the proper task for Christian communities, which should not abandon their responsibilities to specialists, no matter how gifted.

As an amateur in film criticism, I take courage from the stupendous trust Paul displayed in the largely uneducated members of early Christian tenement churches and house churches in Rome—to carry forward the tasks of discernment that ancient cultures otherwise reserved for highly trained experts, as do modern cultures today. To take up the challenge of Paul's approach with regard to contemporary films would be to demonstrate the "force of the gospel," which is the theme of our next chapter. I am confident that when people undertake this task, their dialogues will also result in significant, fresh insights about the bearing of biblical texts on the days ahead.

Selecting the Movies

The following chapters bring Pauline texts into conversation with movies that have either proven to be significant for large numbers of people or have particular cultural significance for the present time. For the most part I have selected films that were not only widely viewed in their first runs but also have been popular as videos. My hope is that most of my readers will have already experienced these films and thus will have an interest in thinking about their religious and ethical significance. One exception to this is *A Separate Peace*, which was not successful as a film; however, the novel continues to be widely read in literature classes. *Empire of the Sun* was not as widely viewed as a film as the others but is often rented in videotape. The opposite, I believe, could be said about *Red Dawn*. Several of the movies discussed are among the most popular of all time, including *Star Wars* and *Amadeus*. Whether one personally enjoys all these films or not, I believe each is significant enough to be brought into the kind of dialogue with Pauline texts that can speak with revelatory power to American culture.

The movement from chapter to chapter follows the path suggested by the shape of Paul's letters, which begin with shared faith experiences and move on to the concrete issues facing a congregation. Chapters 2 through 5 deal with Paul's basic beliefs in connection with four provocative films. The theme of "the Force" in *Star Wars* relates closely to Paul's definition of the gospel, throwing new light on the standards that might be employed in discerning the contemporary implications of other films. His idea of sin as suppression of the truth is embodied in *Amadeus*, which proves to be widely applicable in the current situation. The implications of Paul's approach to Adam's fall relates to *A Separate Peace*, throwing new light on widely shared American beliefs. God's mysteriously merciful self-revelation is manifest in *Tender Mercies*, throwing light on Paul's approach to resurrection and justification.

Chapters 6 through 8 deal with Paul's theme of being "all things to all people." The possibility of righteous people emerging from among the "Gentiles" is correlated with *Grand Canyon*, which suggests how urban disorder might be understood. The need for empathy concerning male and female roles is addressed in the chapter related to *Tootsie*, using a passage in 2 Corinthians concerning comfort in the midst of afflictions. Then *Ordinary People* comes into dialogue with Paul's view that all persons are "earthen vessels" rather than perfect performers. Chapters 9 through 11 take up ethical guidelines. Paul's distinction between "supermindedness" and "sobermindedness" is correlated with *Empire of the Sun*, allowing new insights to surface concerning the current state of American civil religion. Paul's warning about "vengeance" throws light on *Pale Rider*, revealing the need for new attitudes toward violence and law enforcement. The apocalyptic basis of Paul's ethic is brought into dialogue with a piece of apocalyptic filmmaking, *Red Dawn*.

The epilogue takes up a text from 2 Timothy that was probably written a generation after Paul's death: here we deal with the result of his becoming "Saint Paul" for those who survived his passing. More importantly, we hear in this passage the admonitions to "reignite the charisma" and to avoid "a spirit of timidity," which not only echo the themes in *Dead Poets Society* but also deserve to be heeded by those interested in relating biblical materials to other contemporary films.

The willingness to become "all things to all people" need not entail an abandonment of intellectual discipline or of critical loyalty to the tradition. As we shall see, there is ample reason to be loyal not only to the classical, theological tradition but also to the new cultural traditions embodied in these movies. It makes sense to become "a slave of all," so that the power of the gospel to transform the world is allowed its full range.

2

Star Wars and "the Force" of Paul's Gospel

For I am not ashamed [of] the gospel:
 it is the force of God for salvation to all who have faith,
both to the Jew first and then to the Greek,
 for in it the righteousness of God is revealed from
 faith to faith,
as it is written,
 "He who through faith is righteous shall live."

(Rom. 1:16–17)

L uke Skywalker, the young superhero of *Star Wars*[1], is
 putting on his flight gear for the climactic battle with
the Death Star that threatens to destroy the last remnants of
a brave rebel force. His somewhat cynical friend, Han Solo,
who is packing a space freighter to escape before the uneven
battle, pauses for a moment and then says with a kind of
awkward voice, "May the Force be with you!"

Skywalker's X-wing fighter then negotiates the dangerous
course along the seamlike corridor on the surface of the giant
space station, the Death Star. He succeeds where more experienced pilots have failed. He turns off his targeting computer
in response to "the Force" addressing him in the voice of his
mentor, Obi Wan Kenobi: "Trust your feelings, Luke!"[2] By

allowing "the Force" to pull the trigger, Luke fires the torpedo that blows the enemy globe into a billion sparkling fragments. Theater and living-room video audiences all over America have cheered this scene. "The Force" has triumphed over evil; good and right have prevailed just in the nick of time. A nuclear blast like that which seems so problematic when used against earthly cities turns out beautifully in the story, restoring peace and honor to a corrupted galaxy.

There is a compelling gospel in this film, one that deserves to be compared with Paul's words in Romans. I speak of "deserving" to be compared, to be taken seriously. Not only is it a great film from the cinematic point of view, because of its brilliant photography, excellent acting, and witty screenplay, but it is also great because of its impact on audiences. Like most popular films in modern America, particularly ones that attract audiences to see them repeatedly, it reveals the formative values of the culture and to some degree forms those values as well. In the years since *Star Wars* was first shown in 1977, its huge audiences have generated some of the largest profits in the history of American film. Millions of Americans have seen it repeatedly. I read a survey several years ago indicating that many people saw it as many as twenty to thirty times. This indicates that a kind of ritual was being experienced. I know from personal observation that there were church families who attended the film a dozen or more times by the early 1980s because *Star Wars* seemed to embody the ultimate Christian value of right triumphing over wrong. It was perceived to be an ideal form of good, clean family entertainment, with authentic religious value. One woman reported to a columnist that she had seen *Star Wars* more than forty times. Every time she got depressed, she would go again, and it would cheer her up.

This kind of filmgoing is more than mere entertainment. It involves a ritualistic reenactment of a story of salvation, comparable to the function of religious rituals studied by anthropologists and theologians. This was certainly not intended by George Lucas, who said he simply wanted to create a modern fairy tale. But judging from its repetitive appeal to many Americans, to say nothing of its symbolic embodiment in the Strategic Defense Initiative during the Reagan era, we are justified in treating the Star Wars gospel with full seriousness. By reflecting on its relationship to the gospel in Romans, we will be able to gain a clearer understanding of each. By moving back and forth on the interpretive arch between the modern and the ancient gospel, we can bring the contours and implications of each more clearly to light for the contemporary audience.

Two Gospels and Two Forms of Salvation

Our starting point is the reference to "the force" in the thesis statement of Romans. Paul writes that "the gospel . . . is the force of God for salvation to all who have faith, both to the Jew first and then to the Greek, for in it the righteousness of God is revealed from faith to faith" (Rom. 1:16–17). Paul speaks first about what the force of the gospel achieves, namely "salvation." The gospel achieves the release of humankind from the threat of sin, death, and the law. The gospel proclaims Christ as the savior who brings freedom to the world through his life, death, and resurrection.

George Lucas's film depicts an Old Republic in a distant galaxy corrupted by "restless, power-hungry individuals within the government, and the massive organs of commerce."[3] An evil conspiracy led by Darth Vader is now seeking total domination of the galaxy, so that salvation requires the miraculous escapes and victories of Princess Leia, Skywalker, Solo, Kenobi, and the two super robots, R2D2 and C3PO. The cosmic scale of the conflict and the ultimate weight of the issue in the film throws light back onto the theme of salvation in Romans, warning against the prevailing interpretive tradition that overlooks such cosmic dimensions.

Despite significant similarities, there are important differences between these two gospels, both in the nature and the means of salvation. For *Star Wars*, it is achieved by laser beam blasters, nuclear torpedoes, and speedy spacecraft. The galaxy is cleansed by the annihilation of the hordes of Stormtroopers. This is the classic American myth of "regeneration through violence,"[4] consistent with the cowboy Westerns and the cops-and-robbers tales that have dominated American popular entertainment. For Paul the means of salvation is the gospel. "The gospel is the force of God for salvation," he writes. What he had in mind was that the good news about God's love shown in Christ has the power, the force, to turn life around. A key issue in Romans is where the true force may be found. Paul insists that it does not lie in the power to destroy adversaries, or in enforcing conformity to a single law, but rather in the message that God's love is unconditional and that the human war against God should therefore cease.

It also follows that the nature of salvation differs substantially in these two gospels. For *Star Wars*, it consists of the restoration of a hierarchical order of princesses and subjects, warriors and traders. It features a relationship with "the Force" that is accessible only to selected warriors and saints like Obi Wan Kenobi, affording them the ability to destroy their enemies.[5] The similarity to European fascism is particularly striking at this point: such warriors have been described as capable of "that magic flash of a moment of supreme intuition" that comes "to the hero and to none other."[6] Lucas defines "the Force" in this heroic sense as "a nothingness that can accomplish miracles"[7] in the sense that it guides the military instinct that can save a civilization from domination by a venal and ruthless horde of oppressors who must be annihilated. The public's participation in this salvation is limited to celebrating its triumph, because they could play only the role of passive spectator in the martial drama. Their participation in "the Force" matches Mussolini's vision: "The Fascist State, the highest and most powerful form of personality, is a force, but a spiritual force, which takes over all the forms of the moral and intellectual life of man."[8]

For Paul, salvation consists of the restoration of an egalitarian order including male and female, slave and free, Greek and Jew, educated and uneducated. It is based on a new relationship that all persons may have with God, based on faith rather than inheritance or merit. It involves freedom from unrighteousness, sin, and death, which afflict everyone. And participation in the "righteousness of God" involves membership in a faith community marked by mutual edification and responsibility. There are no passive spectators and no incorrigible enemies in the new age established by Paul's gospel, because it calls everyone into accountability and transformation.

So the first question our comparison poses is this: which gospel, which form of salvation is more humane and healthy? Is it the flashing light sabers and nuclear blasters of *Star Wars*? That kind of salvation promises that the differently attired adversaries will disappear from the scene. The alternative that Paul offers is a gospel of the impartial love and justice of God that comes to friend and foe alike. This gospel is most powerfully experienced when people experience weakness and defeat. So which kind of salvation does this world really need?

The Target of Salvation

Paul draws the target circle very large in his letter to the Romans: "the gospel . . . is the force of God for salvation *to every one* who has faith, to the Jew first and also to the Greek" (Rom. 1:16, RSV, emphasis mine). This formulation includes the opposing groups, which tended to view each other as enemies. There were widely shared feelings of cultural and religious superiority in Paul's time between Jews and Greeks. Each side was proud of its superiority over the other; each tended to view its adversaries as degenerate, wicked, and stupid. It is similar to the ethnic hostility that is surfacing all over the world, now that the era of the Cold War no longer holds such impulses in check. Evidence of such hostilities surfaces at a number of points in Paul's letter to the Romans. Yet Paul refrains from taking sides. The salvation of which he speaks is for *everyone*, the good folks and the bad folks, from whichever side you prefer to set the equation. Each side needs to be transformed by internalizing the challenging gospel.

Part of the appeal of *Star Wars*, of course, is that only the bad folks are targeted for blast-gun salvation. A few of the virtuous rebels are killed, to be sure, in the course of the battle. But the film does not allow anyone with whom the audience has developed a close attachment to be killed or mutilated. When the old Jedi knight Kenobi is killed in the light-saber duel with Darth Vader, it is because he crosses his arms and gives up his life willingly to distract attention from the escaping spaceship carrying his friends. And he reappears as the voice of "the Force" in the climactic torpedo scene. There is no sadness in his death, only a certainty that "the Force" has somehow prevailed.

In contrast, Darth Vader, the Grand Moff Tarkin, and their Nazi-attired cohorts are targeted from the beginning for destruction. A reviewer in *The Christian Century* describes our reactions as viewers: "though we continually teeter with Luke and Han on the abyss of death, we know from repeated forays into this region that things are going to work out all right, that Grand Moff Tarkin and Darth Vader will be defeated and the salutary order of the republic restored."[9] This is appealing not only because good wins out in the end but because we identify with the heroes and heroine. We take comfort that they do not have to change, or suffer unduly, or receive the brunt of the peculiar means of salvation in the film—nuclear annihilation.

This narrow targeting of salvation is great—so long as the right side wins the super bowl, so to speak. There is something very partisan about the *Star Wars* religion, and the system only holds up so long as the team one identifies with wins. If it is defeated, the entire system collapses, bringing "the Force" right down with it.

Paul's gospel is more fair-minded and impartial. His insistence that the gospel "is the force of God for salvation" and is for "everyone," both Jews and Greeks, is also more democratic. Paul resists the pretensions of those who feel superior. He assumes there is no cosmic force weighing the scales to the advantage of the home team. Whereas Lucas's film has princesses and hereditary senators who naturally take control because they are superior to others, Paul holds to the equality of all persons before God. In the film, this question of equality is particularly clear with regard to religious abilities. Only the Jedi knights are pictured as really understanding "the Force." As Kenobi told Luke while the young knight was in training, "Knowledge of the Force and how to manipulate it was what gave the Jedi his special power." In this first of the *Star Wars* films, even Princess Leia seems to be excluded from this extraordinary ability.

The contrast with Paul's premise is marked: "To each is given the manifestation of the Spirit for the common good" (1 Cor. 12:7, RSV). Paul was convinced that the force of the spirit was given to all Christians as they used their abilities and gifts for building up the body of Christ. The inclusive quality of this Pauline orientation will be developed in relation to the movies *Tootsie* and *Ordinary People* in subsequent chapters of this study.

This emphasis on equality is carried out in Romans with a powerful realism. In contrast to the claims of Greeks and Jews, religious or secular persons, Paul shows in the first three chapters of Romans that everyone falls short. People cannot rely on their accomplishments when facing the holiness of God. Victorious battles melt away into nothing before the holy love revealed in Christ, so that in the end all must affirm what Paul proclaims about the human race: "For there is no distinction; since all have sinned and fall short of the glory of God . . ." (Rom. 3:23, RSV). This doctrine of the impartiality of God is central for the entire argument of the letter to the Romans.[10] This means that each person on earth needs salvation. Everyone becomes a target of Paul's gospel. And all may become recipients of that salvation if they open themselves to its force.

The Cosmic Scale of Redemption

When Paul's gospel overcomes partial vision, breaking down arrogant feelings that particular groups deserve favoritism, then and only then does the cosmic dimension of redemption become a reality. His claim in Romans is that the gospel is the force of God in which "the righteousness of God" is revealed. That is, God restores the creation to its righteous order and harmony when the gospel succeeds in bringing rebellious persons to salvation. In the words of commentator Ernst Käsemann, the reference to divine righteousness "speaks of the God who brings back the fallen world into the sphere of his legitimate claim."[11] There is a cosmic scope of redemption in this sentence that matches the cosmic scale of the battle in *Star Wars*. In Paul's case, the spread of the gospel message is viewed as a decisive phase in the revelation of God's righteousness, restoring individuals, groups, and the creation itself. This is why the verb is in the present tense: "the righteousness of God *is* revealed." Commentator James Dunn is on target in suggesting that "Paul's experience of evangelizing the Gentiles gives him firm confidence that in the gospel as the power of God to salvation such early converts are being given to see the righteousness of God actually happening, taking effect in their own conversion."[12]

A clearer grasp of the theme of divine righteousness in Romans allows us to see the thematic link with *Star Wars* more clearly. A healthy yearning for cosmic righteousness is central for the film. The Old Republic destroyed by the evil conspirators on Darth Vader's death ship had been marked by peace and justice. The Jedi knights "for over a thousand generations" had been "the guarantors of peace and justice in the Old Republic" until they were "exterminated through treachery and deception," to quote from the novel based on the film.[13] The ascetic old Kenobi, the last of the Jedi, passed on their passion for righteousness to the young Sky-walker: "Remember, Luke, the suffering of one man is the suffering of all. Distances are irrelevant to injustice. If not stopped soon enough, evil eventually reaches out to engulf all men, whether they have opposed it or ignored it." This eloquent call for righteousness resonates with American and British political rhetoric in the recent generation, and part of the enormous appeal of *Star Wars* is in allowing us to imagine such goodness to triumph. This contributes to the ritual effect of the film for persons who want to see it over and over again: it rehearses the vivid triumph of righteous-ness over wickedness, thus fulfilling a very real need in au-diences.

Reflecting on the relationship with Romans helps to ar-ticulate the dilemma—that such visions rarely seem to match reality. Quests for absolute righteousness that begin with violence and assume that someone else is a justifiable target usually end up in disaster. All over the world in re-cent years we see this kind of righteousness resulting in suf-fering and pain—in the torture chambers of Argentina, Iran, and Iraq; in the death camps of Uganda, Cambodia, and Bosnia; on the battlefields of Lebanon, Afghanistan, and the Persian Gulf; on the streets of Northern Ireland and the jun-gles of Nicaragua and El Salvador. The *Star Wars* approach to righteousness tends to lead each participant to certainty that triumph through the elimination of the enemy will re-store peace and justice.

In view of recent history, Paul's message about the gospel as the means by which God regains righteous rule over the world offers a viable alternative. The righteousness of God revealed in the cross of Christ marks the final judg-ment on zealotism. It stands against narrow definitions and partisan loyalties. It transcends economic, social, and politi-cal systems. It lays claim to every area of life, from family re-lations to political preferences, from leisure-time activities to daily labors. The righteousness of God implies a divine will to regain control over a corrupted creation, thereby restoring the very environment that humans have defaced through exploitation and war, recovering its originally intended beauty and balance.

How is this to be achieved? Paul says it is a matter of leading the world by means of the gospel toward genuine "faith." The gospel is "the force of God for salvation to all who have faith, . . . for in it the righteousness of God is revealed from faith to faith." The usual explanation is that faith is a matter of holding fast to the gospel concerning the love of God, living in response to its word of mercy, and thus enjoying a proper relation to God. If the fall of humankind was the result of human pride in trying to act like arrogant gods, defining good and evil for themselves, the restoration comes when humans accept their limitations and live in faith as sons and daughters near the heart of their divine parent. This explanation firmly grasps the individualistic dimension of faith but tends to overlook that the expression "from faith to faith" within the context of the thesis of Romans implies participation in faith communities.[14] Paul hoped that the gospel would spread through the establishment of Christian cells that would become the beachheads of righteousness in a fallen world. In these small groups, living together in the tenement spaces of Rome and in the house churches provided by patrons, Christians would share their food and resources, cooperate in facing the challenges of maintaining families in a difficult urban environment, and participate in the mission to the ends of the world. In contrast to the almost exclusively individualistic understanding of faith and salvation in modern Christianity, Paul refers here to the creation of a tolerant, inclusive, and responsible society sustained by early Christian churches. In the radically egalitarian life of such churches, the originally intended righteousness of God was to be lived out, which could transform the world.

The Gospel and the Movies

Could the "force" of Paul's gospel become a significant resource in approaching the other movies of our time? His idea of the righteous living "through faith" (Rom. 1:17) involved communities of faith being guided by the gospel. As we noted in the last chapter, Paul's admonitions about not conforming to the world and ascertaining the will of God were addressed to communities rather than to individuals. He trusted the process of discussion and group evaluation, informed by the gospel, to determine what was the "good and acceptable and perfect" (Rom. 12:2, RSV). We find the same reliance on communal evaluation when he urges the Thessalonians to "test everything; hold fast to what is good; abstain from every form of evil" (1 Thess. 5:21, RSV). Even in connection with inspired utterances, Paul urges: "Let two or three prophets speak, and let the others weigh what is said" (1 Cor. 14:29, RSV). The process seems comparable to groups of friends or class members gathering to discuss an inspired film. It requires the intellectual, emotional, moral, and spiritual resources of transformed groups to come to terms with materials as potent as contemporary movies.

It is this rational, communal dimension that is conspicuously missing in *Star Wars*. It relies on the leadership of royalty and the martial instinct of an inspired few rather than on public, moral reflection as the keys to action. Skywalker is instructed to pull the visor down over his eyes and thus to rely on pure intuition while dueling with the light saber. "You must try to divorce your actions from conscious control," Kenobi tells him. "You must cease cogitation, relax, stop thinking."[15] The idea is that "the Force" will guide the knight through pure instinct to strike home at the right instant, killing his adversary. In an earlier conversation Kenobi had explicitly identified "the Force" with "instinct" while describing Luke's father as the "best pilot I ever knew . . . and a smart fighter. The Force . . . the instinct was strong in him."[16] The celebration of this martial capacity is reminiscent of Mussolini's words:

> My program is action, not thought. . . . We think with our blood.[17]

> War alone brings up to their highest tension all human energies and puts the stamp of nobility upon the peoples who have the courage to meet it.[18]

I am not implying that George Lucas consciously intended to recommend this kind of fascist ideology. We may be dealing with unintended implications here. And there are some who interpret this instinctual aspect of "the Force" within the framework of some proper form of religious mysticism. But one thing is clear: the issue of group rationality and discernment raised by *Star Wars* needs to be clarified if people are going to enter into a healthy discussion of films and biblical texts.

I believe the Pauline gospel is more adequate than the *Star Wars* gospel, in part because it encourages and sustains the resources of the many rather than the few. The kind of righteousness that can redeem the world "is revealed from faith to faith" (Rom. 1:17), from person to person and group to group. The gospel calls us to enter into the charged arena of magical images and stories that shape our culture, discerning together how peace and honor may truly be restored to a corrupted galaxy. May the force be with us!

3

Amadeus:
Sin, Salvation, and Salieri

For I have already established that Jews as well as Greeks are all
under sin.
   As it is written,
      "There is none righteous, not one;
         there is no one that understands,
         there is no one that seeks God.
            All turn aside,
            together they are corrupted;
         there is no one that does what is proper,
         there is not a single one."
            "An open grave is their throat,
         their tongues deceive."
            "The poison of asps is under their lips."
            "Whose mouth is full of curses and bitterness."
            "Their feet are quick to shed blood,
            ruin and misery are in their paths,
            and the path of peace they do not know."
            "There is no fear of God before their eyes."[1]

(Rom. 3:9–18)

For the wrath of God is being revealed from heaven
   against all impiety and wickedness of humans
      who by wickedness are suppressing the truth.

(Rom. 1:18)

Isuspect that the creators of the Academy Award–winning film *Amadeus*[2] would be surprised to read this essay. There is no evidence that they consciously intended to express Paul's theory of sin and forgiveness. This is one of those rare and inspired films that embodies truth beyond the grasp of filmmaker and playwright, conveying a distinctive and little-understood aspect of the theology of Romans. At first glance, the conventional sense of sin as indecency seems to match Wolfgang Amadeus Mozart pretty well. The film depicts Mozart as an arrogant and uncouth genius who was admired but ultimately hated by the court composer, Antonio Salieri. Mozart's foul-mouthed jokes, his sexual irresponsibility, his inability to live within the limits of his income or time, his chronic abuse of alcohol—all of these made him irritating to conventional morality.[3] His father was depicted as furious with his irresponsibility; his archbishop was disgusted at his arrogance; and the advisors of Emperor Joseph were alarmed at the young composer's blithe violations of political conformity and social etiquette. According to the dictionary definition of sin as "the willful or deliberate violation of some religious or moral principle," Mozart would seem to qualify as a rake of the first order.

A very different perspective emerges when one views *Amadeus* in the light of Romans 1 and 3. It is the character of Mozart's well-placed and highly successful competitor, the composer Salieri, that reveals the deeper, and ultimately more pervasive and serious level of sin that Paul has in mind.

Sin as Suppression of the Truth

The well-known passage in Romans (3:9–25) opens with a shockingly sweeping allegation: "I have already charged," Paul states, "that all humans, Jews as well as Greeks, are under sin" (v. 9). The term "sin" is used here in the singular, implying that a single, alienating power has all humans in its grip.[4] The Revised Standard Version translation adds the word "power" to this sentence in order to make this clear: "under the power of sin." Karl Barth explained this expression with the following words: "Both Jews and Greeks, the sons of God and the natural children of the world, are . . . children of wrath. They are, without exception, in subjection to the foreign power of sin. . . . To us God is, and remains, unknown; we are, and remain, homeless in this world; sinners we are and sinners we remain."[5]

Paul had described the shape of this universal sin in the earlier chapters of his letter to the Romans. All human beings, he argued, have an innate capacity to recognize God in the created order, but we "suppress" this truth (Rom. 1:18) and worship ourselves instead. One commentator suggests the vivid translation, "hold the truth imprisoned."[6] The term used here has the sense of "hold down" or "suppress,"[7] the explicit effort to distort reality. We exchange "the truth about God for a lie and worship and serve the creature rather than the Creator" (Rom. 1:25). When this occurs, Paul contends, the human capacity to distinguish the truth is crippled. "So they are without excuse," Paul writes, "for although they knew God they did not honor him as God or give thanks to him, but they became vain in their thinking and their senseless heart was darkened. Claiming to be wise, they became witless" (Rom. 1:20–21). Whenever humans place themselves rather than God at the center of the universe, they inevitably begin to lie about it, suppressing the realization of what they have done. C. K. Barrett describes the link between such suppression and a false self-image: "The immediate result of this rebellion was a state of corruption in which men were no longer capable of distinguishing between themselves and God, and accordingly fell into idolatry, behind which, in all its forms, lies in the last resort the idolization of the self."[8] In this way human beings come under a power so invisible, so unconscious, and yet so encompassing in its evil consequences that they cannot grasp what has gone wrong. This is how all humans fall "under the power of sin," to use the expression of our text.

This brings us to the character of Salieri in this Milos Forman film, which is much closer to the thought of Paul than in Peter Shaffer's original play.[9] The film tells us that, years before he met Mozart, the young Salieri as a boy had prayed to God, "Make me great . . . make me famous through the world. Make me immortal. Let everyone speak my name with love. After I die, let them repeat my name ever with love. In return, I promise you . . . my chastity . . . my industry . . . and my deep humility."[10] Shortly after this bargain, Salieri's father died by choking on a fish bone and the lad was free to pursue his musical career. Ultimately he became the most famous composer in Vienna.

The conventional shape of Salieri's Christian dedication disguised what Romans refers to as worshiping and serving "the creature rather than the Creator." To achieve immortality as a composer or in any other field is to become more than a creature. That everyone should speak our name with love is something only God deserves. As Samuel Terrien describes the depiction of Salieri in the play, "He sought 'to snatch the Absolute.' He knew, of course, that the Absolute belongs to God alone, but that is precisely the target of his craving, 'to blaze like a comet across the firmament of Europe.'"[11] However, the realization of the true nature of Salieri's arrogant yearning for eternal popularity was suppressed under the disguise of piety. He was caught in the net of the "tradesmen" view of "the God of Bargains" who will guarantee divine favor in return for human devotion: "You give me so—I'll give you so! No more, no less!"[12]

The entire campaign that Salieri later mounted to frustrate the career of Mozart is comprehensible in light of Paul's analysis of the "power of sin." The older composer had been deeply impressed by the originality and power of Mozart's music. When he examined some pages of Mozart's compositions, he said with amazement that they revealed "no correction of any kind. The music was already finished . . . in his head. Page after page, as if he were taking dictation! And what music, finished as no music was ever finished! Take away one note, and it would be diminished. Take away one phrase, and the structure would fall. . . . This was the very voice of God."

But Salieri found it outrageous that the uncouth Mozart should have been selected as the "instrument" capable of expressing this divine level of music. "All I ever wanted was to sing to God," Salieri complained after Mozart had humiliated him by instantly memorizing and then improving a little march he had written for the emperor to welcome Mozart: God "gave me that longing. But why impress me with the desire, like a lust in my body, and then deny me the talent?"

Later Salieri discovered that Mozart had had an affair with the beautiful opera singer whom Salieri secretly admired. "The creature has had my darling girl," he declares with bitterness. That God would allow such a thing was incomprehensible. For the first time in Salieri's life, he began to know hatred, to think "violent thoughts." After discovering the full scope of Mozart's creative power, Salieri declares war on the God who had selected this monster as his vehicle. Taking down the wooden crucifix in his chamber and placing it in the fireplace, he declares to God: "From now on we are enemies, you and I. Because you choose for your instrument a boastful, lustful, smutty, infantile boy, and you leave me only the ability to recognize your incarnation . . . you are unjust, unfair, unkind. I will block you, I swear it. I will hinder and harm your creature on earth. As far as I am able, I will ruin your incarnation."

Salieri hires a maid to serve in Mozart's cluttered apartment so Salieri could spy out what his competitor was doing and discredit his compositions before they appeared. While appearing to be Mozart's friend and protector, Salieri saw to it that Mozart's magnificent operas were given short runs in the court theater. Finally, he contrived a plan to haunt Mozart by wearing the black mask that Wolfgang's deceased father had used in a masquerade party. The masked Salieri offers a large fee for Mozart to write a requiem that Salieri could usurp and perform as his own creation at the funeral of his competitor. It was, as Salieri put it, "a way, a terrible way, in which I could triumph over God." The unfair Deity who poured his divine music into this scatological nerd, Mozart, would finally be mocked and defeated.

So it was that a person whose conventional devotion disguised the lust for immortal status ended up under the "power of sin," displaying what Paul described at the end of chapter 1 of Romans in terms of the consequences of suppressing the truth: "And since they did not see fit to acknowledge God, God gave them up to a base mind and to improper conduct. They were filled with all manner of wickedness, evil, covetousness, malice. Full of envy, murder, strife, deceit, malignity . . ." (Rom. 1:28–29, RSV). The attempt to manipulate God was really an assault on deity itself, resulting in a distortion of Salieri's humanity. In Terrien's words, "Because the religious man feels deceived, his belief turns into blasphemy. Because the moral man feels cheated, his virtue becomes the trough of malevolence."[13]

Mozart's Strategies of Suppression

It would be tempting in the light of Salieri's sin to interpret Mozart as a genuine embodiment of humane piety. There was an innocence and integrity in his music and outlook that seemed to be immune to the manipulative, conforming, and suppressed sins of everyone else in the film. He did not allow the silly tastes and standards of his time to throttle the creative urge that he felt. When the Emperor Franz Joseph II echoes the director's complaint about *The Abduction from the Seraglio* as having "too many notes," Mozart remains true to what he has created. "There are just as many notes, Majesty, as are required. No more, no less." The idiotic emperor replies that Mozart should not be discouraged. His opera was "quality work, and there are simply too many notes, that's all. Just cut a few, and it will be perfect." Mozart replies, "Which few did you have in mind, Majesty?"

Mozart remains the free spirit in this film, making music for the pure joy of the creative process. This corresponds to the reason Karl Barth was able to celebrate him as the purest expression of creatureliness.[14] Knowing the wide range of life's joys and sorrows, Mozart always remains within his creaturely limits. Barth writes, "Granted, darkness, chaos, death, and hell do appear, but not for a moment are they allowed to prevail. Knowing all, Mozart creates music from a mysterious center, and so knows and observes limits to the right and the left, above and below. He maintains moderation."[15]

Yet the film *Amadeus* is honest enough to portray a side of Mozart that parallels Salieri's flaws. The cocky young man refuses to submit his music to the panel of judges in order to earn the lucrative position of teaching the emperor's niece. He tells the court chamberlain that in comparison with the other composers who might apply, "They may be better qualified, but I'm the best." Having fallen prey to pride, Mozart is depicted as being frustrated when he failed to gain the public recognition that more conforming composers like Salieri enjoyed. He expressed his sense of deprivation in life by indulging in too much drinking and partying, falling into a dissolute life-style that contributed to exhaustion and finally to his death.

In a sense, Mozart was involved in his own unique form of worshiping and serving "the creature rather than the Creator," to use Paul's words (Rom. 1:25). He violated his creaturely limitations.[16] For instance, he childishly hoped to retain the affection of the singer he had seduced while going ahead with marriage to Constanza. He foolishly denied his chronic indebtedness while bounding off to yet another expensive diversion. Responding to his father's query about his financial situation, Mozart says, "It's marvelous. They love me here" in Vienna. He refused to accept limits to his spending, his drinking, or his carousing. While he understood the threat such behavior posed to his life, having experienced it in the wrath of his father and embodied it in the opera *Don Giovanni,* where exploitative behavior earns the reward of hell, Mozart failed to recognize his own condition.

In the end, *Amadeus* suggests Mozart was as entangled by his strategies of suppressing the truth as was Salieri. Yet for him as for every other human, the truth will finally come out, sometimes in death-dealing ways. Could this be the deeper meaning of the hyenalike laugh that Tom Hulce affected in his portrayal of Mozart? Was it perhaps an expression of the attempt to relieve the tension between the truth one wishes to suppress and the truth that one knows will some day be revealed? At any rate, one thing is clear: while Mozart's music is as immortal as any ever composed, his life proved fragile indeed.

The cinematic version of *Amadeus* drives us therefore to hear Romans with sharpened ears. "What then? Are we Jews any better off?" Are we law abiding, hard working, and disciplined Salieris any better off than the dissolute Mozart? Are we creative, nonconformist Mozarts really immune to the sins of the Salieris of this world? "No, not at all," says Paul with relentless logic, "for I have already established" that all humans, both Jews and Greeks, are under the power of sin (Rom. 3:9). Each human being on this earth is similar in this regard. Humans react to the experience of vulnerability by pretending to be divine. From the time of infancy, human beings seek the secure status that only God can ever have, expressing their lust for prestige with countless strategies of differentiating themselves from others. People make their bargains with a shopkeeper god, seeking the kind of uncritical admiration and permanent achievement that humans can never finally achieve. But they suppress the truth about what they have done, and then set about to suppress all competition. Blind to the human condition, unconscious of their final motivations, and hence under "the power of sin," Americans as well as others fit the description that Paul contrived by arranging and adapting a series of citations from the Hebrew scriptures.[17] In the text of Romans 3:9–12 quoted at the head of this chapter, the corruption is said to be universal. It leads, as in *Amadeus*, to deception and death.

Grace Subverts the Strategies of Suppression

So is there no hope for human beings? Will our suppression of the truth about God and ourselves go on until all of us are with Mozart, in an unmarked grave, or with Salieri, in the insane asylum? Is there no way to avoid such gruesome fates, no chance of recognition by which we can come to terms with our particular form of suppression?

The good news at the heart of Romans is that the grace of God conveyed in Christ is able to restore humans to righteousness, breaking the power of sin. "Since all have sinned and fall short of the glory of God, they are made righteous by his grace as a gift, through the redemption which is in Christ Jesus" (Rom. 3:23–24). Behind this abstract language is a powerful event of unconditional acceptance that is open to everyone. Paul had discovered this in the cross of Christ. To him the cross revealed human suppression at its height and divine forgiveness at its depth. The political and religious leaders who crucified Jesus epitomized the human effort to suppress the truth about God and themselves. When people encounter what is truly good and noble, their deepest instinct is to stamp it out, to crucify him, so that they can remain alone, unchallenged at the center of the universe. Paul's persecution of the early Christians enacted his strategy of legalistic suppression.

The apostle discovered that the depth of love revealed in Christ was a force capable of penetrating his strategies of suppression. It led him to know that he was acceptable to God even if he was not perfect, not godlike in his powers, not loved and admired by the world. This led to Paul's proclamation that Christ accepts sinners precisely as they are, which overcomes the bitterness and disappointment and alienation people in his time felt—just as they do today—because life had not provided the popularity and success they expected.

Once people begin to internalize this acceptance through faith in the grace of God, they are enabled to see for the first time the enormity of their godlike pretensions. The suppression of the truth about themselves and God lets up for a moment, and they admit that they shall always remain vulnerable, and that God alone is God. In such an instant, the deepest level of forgiveness is possible, because people are confronting not the little mistakes and failures of their lives, but rather the "power of sin" to which they have given themselves in their mad quests to stand at the center of the world. Unconditional grace enables people to experience what Paul calls the "righteousness of God, because in his divine forbearance he had passed over former sins" (Rom. 3:25). Forgiveness is the only power that ultimately can break the "power of sin." It subverts the strategies of suppression, rendering them unnecessary.

In this connection the film *Amadeus* lives up to the implication of its title, "God-loves," designating someone beloved by God.[18] The selection of Mozart's middle name as the title of both the play and the film is not explained in any of the discussions I have seen, yet it is remarkably apt as a description of the impact of the music itself. Salieri described the impression made on him by the closing scene of Mozart's *The Marriage of Figaro*. Having been caught in an effort to initiate an affair, the count asks the forgiveness of his wife. The tender music Mozart wrote for this scene conveyed in Salieri's words "true forgiveness, filling the theater, conferring on all who sat there perfect absolution." The magnificent melody flowed on, "unstoppable," overwhelming every obstacle until perfect reconciliation was achieved. "It was a miracle," Salieri said with amazement. Similarly, Terrien tells us, in the Requiem Mozart manages to convey "a God who accepts and receives the sinner unconditionally. His love is absolutely different from human expectations. . . . Mozart's

Kyrie Eleison is not . . . a somber supplication for forgiveness. The mercy has already come."[19]

Although he was unable to understand it at the time, the film has Salieri encounter the miracle of personal forgiveness moments before he triumphs over Mozart and Mozart's creator. While taking Mozart's final dictation of the Requiem with the diabolical intent of using it at the funeral to mock the God who placed his genius in such an unworthy vehicle, Salieri is stunned when the exhausted composer stops and thanks him. "I thought you did not appreciate my music," Mozart confesses to his unacknowledged adversary. "Please, forgive me," Mozart says.

The theme of mutual forgiveness as a means of coming to terms with finitude is what holds the opening and closing of this powerful film together. In this regard also, the film is much more true to the Pauline vision of the human heart than was the original play by Peter Shaffer. The opening words of the film are spoken behind the closed door of Salieri's bedroom, years after the death of his adversary. "Forgive me, Mozart!" he cries. Having apparently come to terms with the error of his long and deadly thwarting of Mozart's life and music, Salieri utters these words and then tries to take his own life. He lives the rest of his years in the Asylum for the Insane in Vienna, brooding over his contest with God.

After relating his life story to a priest, Salieri at the end of the film accompanies the shocked cleric to the entrance of the asylum. The elderly composer moves through the corridors filled with the mentally ill, dispensing absolution and forgiveness to all the "mediocrities" incarcerated there. Although this closing scene has elements of mockery of traditional religion,[20] it rings true to the theology of Romans. Human beings *are* mediocre when compared with truly godlike qualities; even the best, like Mozart, are vulnerable and flawed, likely to burn out their lives in frustration and self-abuse when they seek to stand at the center of the world. The rest, like Salieri, disguise their frustration in envy of those more successful than themselves, acting out scripts of mutual destruction. The interplay between Paul's letter and this European story exposes a dimension of the human situation that many Americans can recognize as true.

What the American soul needs is absolution. But we need it in the context of facing the truth about ourselves. Until our individual and cultural strategies of suppression are exposed and acknowledged, no one can receive forgiveness at redemptive level. In fact until that happens, the theology of grace that has been so widely preached in North America can be genuinely corrupting, feeding our cultural narcissism and sustaining our strategies of suppression. But when forgiveness, absolution—the experience of unconditional grace—is genuinely and profoundly experienced, it is capable of releasing individuals and societies from the compulsion to suppress the truth about themselves and their life together. Grace alone can break the "power of sin." And when it does, people are enabled to become agents of reconciliation for others, dispensing absolution to those around them, not because they have earned such a privilege, but because they have been redeemed by grace. Along with the rest of the human race, we Americans are all Amadeuses, if we could only recognize it: beloved by God despite all our pretensions and disguises.

Several lines written during the period depicted in the film are a fitting conclusion to this story. Charles Wesley had experienced what Paul proclaims in Romans, and wrote these words: Christ

> breaks the power of cancelled sin,
>> he sets the prisoner free;
> his blood can make the foulest clean,
>> his blood avails for me.[21]

And even for Salieri!

4

A Separate Peace with Adam's Fall

Therefore, having been set right by faith, let us have peace
with God through our Lord Jesus Christ,
     through whom we also have received access by faith
          to this grace in which we have stood.
Let us also boast in the hope of the glory of God.[1]

(Rom. 5:1–2)

It follows that as the sin came into the world through one person,
     and through sin came death,
and thus death came to all persons,
     because all sinned—.
For sin was in the world before law,
     but sin is not put to account when law does not exist.

(Rom. 5:12–13)

For as by the disobedience of one person many were made to
be sinners,
     so also through the obedience of one many will be made
     righteous.
But law slipped in so that the transgression might be
increased;
     but where the sin increased, the grace abounded to the
     ultimate degree,

in order that as the sin reigned in the death,
   so also the grace might reign through righteousness to
   eternal life
      through Jesus Christ our Lord.

(Rom. 5:19–21)

L et us start off with a frank admission. The idea of a fallen human race is not very popular with most Americans, captured as we are by the dream of perfectibility. Since the time of our Declaration of Independence, we have thought of ourselves as belonging to the "New Order of the Ages," to use the motto emblazened in Latin on our currency. Our literature and politics have often celebrated what Richard W. Lewis termed the American Adam,[2] a dream of perfection in a new world unfettered by the traditions of the past. One thinks of John Adams's letter to Thomas Jefferson in 1813: "Many hundred years must roll away before we shall be corrupted. Our pure, virtuous, public spirited, federative republic will last forever, govern the globe and introduce the perfection of man."[3] These sentiments express with embarrassing clarity the essential convictions that millions of Americans still hold about their country, especially in moments of celebration. They resonate with the sense that the narrator, Gene, expresses in John Knowles's story *A Separate Peace*,[4] which was made into a movie in 1972.[5] Gene wakes up with his friend Phineas after spending a night on the beach. They have escaped from summer school on their bicycles, and this is the first dawn Gene has ever witnessed. He describes its surprisingly white purity: "The beach shed its deadness and became a spectral gray-white, then more white than gray, and finally it was totally white and stainless, as pure as the shores of Eden."[6]

Phineas's Exemption from the Fall

The dream of recovering the perfection of Eden, of side-stepping Adam's fall, is what links this classic American story with our text from Romans. The movie is set at Devon Academy, a prep school in New England, where the students are seeking "a separate peace," far from the violence and destruction of World War II. They devise games and contests that break some of the school's rules, including daring one another to jump from a huge tree into the river, expressing their freedom from the terrible events being reported in the news. Their leader, the athlete Phineas, played by John Heyl, seems to be the archetypal American Adam before the fall—fearless, vigorous, serene, and innocent.[7] As Gene reflects on his friend's character after his death, he says Phineas "possessed an extra vigor, a heightened confidence in himself, a serene capacity for affection which saved him. Nothing as he was growing up at home, nothing at Devon, nothing even about the war had broken his harmonious and natural unity."[8] In contrast to the other fellows, who feel guilty about breaking the rules of the prep school, Phineas's vibrant sense of life simply overcomes such petty boundaries. He skips class at the slightest pretext, much in the spirit of the delightful film *Ferris Bueller's Day Off.* Phineas—"Finny"—breaks the dress code with such disarming innocence that he invariably gets away with it. His freedom from fear contributes to outstanding athletic achievements, but here especially Finny's attitude is noncompetitive. "Finny never permitted himself to realize that when you won they lost. That would have destroyed the perfect beauty that was sport. Nothing bad ever happened in sports; they were the absolute good."[9]

It seems, in short, that Phineas escapes Adam's fall. He appears to confirm the essential truth in the American dream of perfectibility. Finny seems to have escaped the sweeping observation that Paul made about the human condition, that "sin" had entered the world through the first human being, Adam, and thus "death came to all persons, because all sinned" (Rom. 5:12). Finny lives in an innocence that strangely rises above conflict and evil, living out "a separate peace" in the midst of a war-torn world. In Gene's words, "Phineas was the essence of this careless peace" of the summer session in 1943,[10] the time when "peace lay on Devon like a blessing, the summer's peace, the reprieve" from the agony and death of an otherwise fallen world. If the story went no further than this, Phineas would simply be a striking exception to Paul's view.

The Poison of Rivalry

With regard to everyone else in the story, *A Separate Peace* confirms Paul's view of Adam's fall. In this passage of Romans, Paul is summarizing a view developed in the book of Genesis, that evil began with the very first man and woman.[11] In the story of Adam and Eve, the ancient Hebrew storytellers developed a precedent of modern concepts of social determinism. The first man and woman, according to the myth, fell from their position in a perfect garden where they had been given satisfying relationships and fulfilling work. The story identifies pride as the motive that caused everything to go awry, with consequences that spread like poison to include all of the future human race.

The key to this story about eating the forbidden fruit from the "tree of the knowledge of good and evil" (Gen. 2:17) is that there were two kinds of knowledge in the story. The story suggests that the man and the woman were given both a positive and a negative command, symbolizing for the Hebrew mind the proper knowledge of good and evil. Their positive command was to "keep the garden," which involved improvement, progress, and mastery. The negative command was to refrain from eating the fruit of a particular tree. But Adam and Eve were not content to remain within these limits. On the premise that they could "become like God, knowing good and evil," they ate the poisoned fruit. They reaped the harvest of pride, both for themselves and their descendants. The story depicts evil spreading like a social poison to corrupt their relationship with each other and with nature, leading to the first murder, and in the later stories in Genesis, to the rise of violent nationalism and war. The problem was that humans desired a second kind of knowledge: not knowledge of creaturely tasks and limits, but a superhuman knowledge by which limits could be abolished forever. Adam's fall came in trying to play god.[12]

Paul picks up this motif of prideful rivalry earlier in Romans 1, where he describes the unwillingness of humans to accept themselves as limited creatures.[13] Although everyone recognizes the "eternal power and deity" of God in the created order (Rom. 1:20), we humans "exchange the truth about God for a lie and worship and serve the creature rather than the Creator" (Rom. 1:25). Rivalry thus lies at the heart of the human dilemma, because humans are uncomfortable with any position less than first. Everyone seeks domination, one way or another, whether as individuals or as nations. The social consequences of this rivalry are visible everywhere, corrupting not only human relationships but even the physical world itself, eroded by greed, choked by pollution, and destroyed by war.

In Romans 5, this concept of social evil is combined with what is ordinarily perceived to be its very opposite: the idea of individual responsibility for evil. When Paul writes that "sin came into the world through one person, and through sin came death, and thus death came to all persons" (Rom. 5:12), he is picking up the theme of social determinism in the Genesis story. When he adds the words "because all sinned," Paul is arguing for individual responsibility. Each person repeats Adam's fall, in one way or another. In the words of Ernst Käsemann, the great German interpreter of Romans, "there is in this verse an ambivalence between destiny and individual guilt."[14] And while philosophers and theologians have argued for one side or the other of this ambivalence between determinism and free will, Paul's effort to unite them is sustained by Knowles's vision in *A Separate Peace*. Unfortunately the cinematic version of the story "resolved the ambiguities and emotional vertigo of the original by casting it as a kind of dark romance," as a

Newsweek writer observed.[15] It is as if the film wanted to re-store the image of Eden at the New England school.[16]

That a kind of social poison of rivalry and hatred in fact had marked Devon Academy despite all its beauty and bitter-sweet memories was one of the discoveries that the narrator made after the tragic events were finished. The relationships in the school were dominated by rivalry and the fear of fail-ure and unpopularity.[17] When Gene returned years after the war to walk up the long white marble flight of stairs where Finny had fallen, "specters seemed to go up and down" with him,[18] memories of fears and failures and even of uncon-scious hatred. Gene had also developed a theory that wars were caused "not by generations and their special stupidities, but . . . instead by something ignorant in the human heart." This ignorant, irrational factor was the expression of rivalry in which nations find themselves "pitted violently against something in the world around them," responding with sav-age destruction.[19]

This insight into the social dimension of Adam's fall de-rived from a more threatening discovery Gene had earlier made about himself. Unlike his friend Phineas, Gene was driven by the rivalry and hatred that were characteristic of the school. He was conscious of how wrong this was, partic-ularly at times when the beauty of New Hampshire over-whelmed him: "in the heady and sensual clarity of these mornings . . . I forgot whom I hated and who hated me. I wanted to break out crying from stabs of hopeless joy . . . because these mornings were too full of beauty for me, be-cause I knew of too much hate to be contained in a world like this."[20] Gene even convinced himself that Phineas was motivated by a similar rivalry. Finny was always suggesting diversions in place of the academic studies in which Gene excelled. So Gene decided, perversely, that it was all an ef-fort to get the better of him. He gained pleasure out of thinking that "we were even after all, even in enmity. The deadly rivalry was on both sides after all."[21] But when Gene discovered that Finny was perfectly willing to let him stay home from one of the escapades to study for a French exam, this comfortable feeling of equality collapsed. In the confused aftermath of this discovery, Gene went to the gigantic tree with his friend for a dangerous leap into the river. He jounced the limb and caused Finny to fall on the hard bank, shattering his leg.

It was only later that Gene was able to bring himself to hint at what had really led him to bounce his best friend out of the tree. "It was just some ignorance inside me, something crazy inside me, something blind, that's all."[22] But the truth had already been more clearly driven home to Gene by another friend at the academy, in themes reminiscent of Genesis and Romans: "You always were a lord of the manor, weren't you? A swell guy, except when the chips were down. You always were a savage underneath . . . like the time you knocked Finny out of the tree." It was rivalry with his best friend that led to the savage act. It was, in fact, Gene's personal repetition of Adam's fateful challenge to Eden's forbidden tree.[23] Refusing to accept limits, and rejecting a relationship in which he was not on top, Gene had crippled his best friend.

How Innocence Courts Death

There is a final theme in this Pauline text that Knowles develops, without of course connecting it explicitly with Romans. The idea that "death" results from sin is prominent both in our text from Romans and in the original creation story in Genesis.[24] The basic issue here is that when people refuse to accept their limitations, they bring death upon themselves and others. Rivalry always seems to have specters on its conscience, and the refusal to acknowledge its presence does nothing but bring death ever more surely.

This leads us back to the question of whether Phineas really had escaped Adam's fall. He had refused to acknowledge the presence of evil, either in the terrible war, or in the behavior of his friends. The movie depicts Gene visiting Finny in his Boston home and admitting that he had intentionally jostled the limb. Finny responds, "I'll kill you if you don't shut up." Gene replied, "You see! Kill me! Now you know what it is! I did it because I felt like that!" As Gene leaves the house, Finny is shown whistling nonchalantly. The truth is too much for him to acknowledge. Later he calls to see if Gene is still "off his rocker."

Months later Phineas returns to school with his shattered leg partially healed, giving up his athletic career. The students have a kind of nocturnal inquest into the cause of the strange accident, making it plain that his best friend, Gene, was responsible. But even now, Phineas is unable to face the truth. He flees blindly out the door to stumble down the long white marble stairs. Later, just before the operation to reset his leg, Phineas again denies the truth to Gene as he reflects back on the dreadful event in the sinister tree: "Something just seized you. It wasn't anything you felt against me, it wasn't some kind of hatred you felt all along. It wasn't anything personal." In fact, it *was* something Gene had felt against his best friend; it *was* a kind of hate; it *was* personal. Adam's fall was as real and direct as Paul had said, and the responsibility thereof was undeniable.

During the operation on Phineas's leg, a bit of bone marrow slips into Finny's bloodstream and his heart stops beating. The American Adam, the embodiment of innocence, is dead. To use the words of our text, "sin came into the world through one person, and through sin came death, and thus death came to all persons."

But was this truly innocence? Did not Phineas die as a consequence of fleeing from the truth about himself and his friend? Did the accident not render him vulnerable to the hate and resentment that afflicted everyone else? Does the film not suggest that the effort to preserve the illusion of innocence is a form of rivalry as lethal as rivalry itself? The truth of this story is that there is no separate peace, no escape from Adam's fall, not for Phineas or anyone else. To deny limitations and the complicity of friends and nation is to court death.

The Gift of Realistic Peace

These insights from John Knowles and the apostle Paul are not intended to lead to despair. Gene was strangely cleansed by recognizing his part in the death of his friend. He was subsequently drafted into the army, but did not become twisted by the savagery of war. He wrote, "I was ready for the war, now that I no longer had any hatred to contribute to it. My fury was gone, I felt it gone, dried up at the source, withered and lifeless. Phineas had absorbed it and taken it with him, and I was rid of it forever."[25] Gene had faced the truth about rivalry corrupting Eden, and he was free from its compulsions.

In a more explicitly theological sense, Paul experienced both unconditional love and the courage to face the truth about his own savagery in his encounter with Christ. Thus our passage begins with the words, "having been set right by faith, let us have peace with God through our Lord Jesus Christ, through whom we also have received access by faith to this grace in which we have stood" (Rom. 5:1).[26] The love of Christ makes people secure enough to recognize their enmity against God, the rage and savagery buried in all polite rivalries.[27] Christ accepted such savagery as a truly innocent man, suffering at the hands of envious and prideful persons. In that death on a cross, people are not only enabled to recognize the truth about themselves but also healed of the buried hostilities that are driving them toward death. Christ has absorbed the hostilities of the human race, and set it free from a deadly legacy.[28]

The human race may thus have "peace with God," a peace that is not a separate peace full of illusions of escaping Adam's fall, but a real peace that comes from acknowledging that all are fallen creatures in need of grace. To live on that grace alone is what genuine Christian perfection is all about. As John Wesley saw it, relying on the grace of Christ allows God to convey an inward peace to troubled hearts. But we should never forget that this is a peace that, like Gene's, renders believers finally ready for war. In one peculiar sense I am content, for instance, that the United Methodist hymnal committee decided in the summer of 1986 to keep "Onward Christian Soldiers" in the hymnal. For if Paul is right, people of faith are called to battle, not against flesh and blood, but against the illusions and distortions of a still fallen world. We who have been touched by the peace of Christ are called to a new type of warfare. We are called to apply pressure against the fallen inclinations of our own country, of the institutions where we work and worship.

Peace and American Political Ideals

What does all this say about the Declaration of Independence and the renewal of the political values that it represents? As a *Chicago Sun-Times* writer commented on the rededication of the Statue of Liberty in 1986, such a celebration is "a communion with the sacred, in which the commitment to particular values is reaffirmed and fortified."[29] It is therefore necessary to examine which values were really being fortified in that celebration. Were they the values and disciplines of a constitutional society committed to defend the interests of the disinherited and thus to provide equality for all? Or were they the values of a separate peace, the conviction of having escaped the evils of the rest of the world and thus ascended to a position of superiority? I think a fair assessment was made by a French journalist who said that "The men who signed the Declaration of Independence in an act of defiance and a cry of liberation would not have understood the meaning of the celebration. . . . It was a self-indulgent, almost isolationistic conformity that prevailed. America has thrown itself a party to celebrate its own greatness, its refound wealth, its renewed patriotism, its infallibility."[30] In the sober light of Paul's assessment of the universal plight of humankind, our nation is called to struggle against the illusion of infallibility that could so easily lead to awesome miscalculations and brutalities.

This does not mean responsible citizens should refuse to celebrate the Fourth of July or sing the national hymns. The institutions of liberty are worth defending, but it is dangerous to believe that America has somehow achieved perfection. The presence of the magnificent lady on Bedloe's Island does not mean that John Adams, Thomas Jefferson, or more recent presidents have somehow arranged a separate peace with Adam's fall. So when we celebrate the glorious gift of freedom, let it be with open eyes and resolute hearts concerning the evils of the present age. Let us celebrate in the firm conviction that the second Adam, our Lord Jesus Christ, has opened the only path to genuine peace— peace with God, and peace with rivals everywhere.

5

The Mysterious God of *Tender Mercies*

I exhort you therefore, brothers [and sisters], through the mercies of God,
> to present your bodies as a sacrifice, living, holy, and
> acceptable to God
>> —your reasonable worship.

(Rom. 12:1)

For this [reason it is] from faith, thus according to grace, that
the promise might be guaranteed to all the descendants, not
only to those of the law but also to those of the faith of Abraham, who is the father of us all, just as it is written that
> "I have made you a father of many nations"
> —in the presence of the God in whom he had faith,
>> who gives life to the dead
>>> and calls that which does not exist into being.

(Rom. 4:16–17)

In the film *Tender Mercies*[1] and in Paul's letter to the Romans, there is a theme of considerable significance for
those who are interested in the mysteries of human restoration. Robert Duvall received an Academy Award for the role
of Mac Sledge, a country singer and composer from Texas.

Down and out after an alcoholic binge, Sledge is taken in as a motel handyman by the young widow Rosa Lee. Tess Harper plays this simple, pious woman whose steadiness and love nurse Sledge back to life. Early in the film, after he begins to regain his vitality, he writes a new song about his estranged daughter. He submits the song to his former manager and receives the message one more time that he is all washed up. Sledge replies with a profane outburst against the world. Rosa Lee replies, "It's bound to be hard on you. . . . I love you," touching his cheek tenderly. "I say my prayers for you and when I thank the Lord for his tender mercies, you're at the head of the list." These words prove significant, because Rosa Lee's prayers are ultimately answered. Mac Sledge finds himself again as a musician and a stepfather.

The reference to God's tender mercies is reminiscent of Paul's letter to the Romans. In the admonition of 12:1, Paul appeals to Christians "through the mercies of God" to live out their lives in service to a world full of people like Mac Sledge, his egocentric and addicted former wife, Dixie, and his doomed daughter, Sue Ann. To live in response to God's mercies links Paul's letter to this screenplay by Texas playwright Horton Foote. But what is of particular interest is that such tender mercies are largely invisible. Both for Paul and for Foote's story, faith is required because the mercies of God are elusive, intangible, and off camera. In a mysterious way, the God of Abraham "gives life to the dead and calls that which does not exist into being," to use the language of Romans 4.

Can people really set their faith in such an elusive God? How can they rely on mercies so ordinary as to be virtually invisible?

The Hidden Story of Mercy

The story of Abraham in Romans 4, just like Sledge's story, centers on the provision of a future through the tender mercies of God. From the perspective of ancient Semites,

Abraham and Sarah had no future because they had grown too old to have a son. As Genesis describes them, "Abram was very rich in cattle, silver and gold. . . . But Sarah, Abram's wife had borne him no children"(Gen. 13:2; 16:1).[2] They were doomed to extinction because their lineage would not pass on to the next generation; their life story would be forgotten when they died; everything they had accomplished in life would be for nought.[3] But Abraham developed a faith that the unseen God of the universe would provide them an heir. He felt that a promise had been given that a son would be born from Sarah's barren womb. Paul makes it plain that there was no proof that such a miracle would occur, and that Abraham had done nothing to guarantee it. He repudiates the rabbinic dogma that "at that time the unwritten law was named among them, and the works of the commandment were then fulfilled."[4] Paul explicitly claims that Abraham's faith did not rest on the fulfillment of a commandment such as circumcision (Rom. 4:10–15). The birth would be a matter of sheer grace, unearned and undeserved. All Abraham had was faith in the promise from this invisible God. It was faith in the future mercies of an elusive deity. Thus Paul insists that the Abraham story is one of "faith, thus according to grace" (Rom. 4:16). The formulation is highly compressed and lacks a subject or verb, allowing a completion such as that suggested by C. K. Barrett: "God's plan was made to rest upon faith in order that it might be a matter of grace."[5] The emphasis is on "the promised inheritance which is achieved by faith and therefore by grace."[6]

At the climax of Abraham and Sarah's story, contrary to all human expectations, the miracle of grace occurred. Sarah conceived and bore a son from whom all the people of Israel ultimately were thought to have descended. Current Christians look back on that event just as Paul did, seeing their inclusion into the people of Abraham's promise as coming through faith as well. Paul felt that the promise came "not only to those of the law [the Jews] but also to those of the faith of Abraham, who is the father of us all [i.e., we Gentiles as well]" (Rom. 4:16). Paul perceived that this story reveals the hidden but universal structure of the new life in Christ enjoyed by Jews and Gentiles alike.[7] In Christ, the tender mercies of God were expressed to everyone on earth. He loved people without their deserving it. Even when they killed him, Jesus said, "Abba, forgive them, for they know not what they do" (Luke 23:34). So for Paul, the death and resurrection of Christ offer each a place in Abraham's promise. Since God's grace comes without people deserving it, they are all potential heirs of Abraham's promised future, recipients of the tender mercies of God that come when there is no reason to expect them. Paul presents this as the hidden plot of every human life.

One reason the film *Tender Mercies* rings true is that it follows this hidden plot. The film opens with a fight scene in a run-down motel room. Mac Sledge emerges from his drunken stupor two days later to face the bright sun in bleak west Texas. The camera makes the "tiny gas station and motel" appear as "a fragile refuge in this wilderness," in the words of film reviewer Richard A. Blake.[8] Sledge admits he can't pay the bill: "Lady, I'm broke." The owner of the tiny motel and gas station, Rosa Lee, gives him work to pay off the bill. She cleans up his filthy room while he picks up debris and fixes screen doors.

Without any dialogue to explain what's on his mind, Sledge indicates he would like to stay on. Rosa Lee offers room, meals, and two dollars an hour. They eat in silence at the end of a day's work. Then Rosa Lee's son, Sunny, asks, "What's your name?" "Mac" is the reply. Sunny asks the visitor, "Did you ever know my daddy?" No. "Would you like him if you did know him?" "Sure."

Soon thereafter the family drives to church, where Sledge is seen next to Sunny singing the hymn. After the service, the pastor greets people at the door of the church. Sunny says he wants to be baptized and the pastor asks Sledge when he was baptized. Sledge says he wasn't. The pastor replies, "We'll have to work on you then." In subsequent scenes Sledge and Rosa Lee begin to talk about their families. Her husband was killed in Vietnam; her father and mother died shortly thereafter. Sledge said he has a daughter, quite a bit older than her son. Sledge is next seen working in the garden, and Rosa Lee appears. He asks her whether she had ever thought about marrying again. She says she has thought about it. He asks her to think about marrying him; she says, "I will think about it." In a later scene, when a new country group comes to meet Sledge, he introduces Rosa Lee as his wife. The gift of love happened off stage, as it were. It is an undeserved grace, a gift of providence from a simple woman who continues to pray for him and to be grateful for him. To quote Richard Blake again, "Mac does nothing to earn love and salvation; these things simply come to him for no apparent reason, as though salvation were his destiny."[9]

Although he refuses to perform because his voice was so used up, Sledge now begins to compose again. He revisits the Opry house where his former wife is performing. Her lyrics deal with the old theme of cheap love: the "best part of all . . . the room at the end of the hall, where everything's made all right." She and her lover can "celebrate the heaven that we've found" in the "best bedroom in town." Sledge is seen in the crowd while she sings about having tried so hard "to keep you off my mind . . . nothing's changed, and I'm still here for the taking." Refusing the allure of this false relationship, Sledge walks out. He returns home to face the loss of his own career, coming very close to betraying his commitment to avoid alcohol. The film allows us to overhear Rosa Lee's prayers during this dark time: "Show me thy way, O Lord, and lead me in thy truth. . . . For salvation do I wait on thee, all the day." This prayer embodies the motif of fidelity that stands at the center of Horton Foote's life and work. Despite all the setbacks in his writing career, he told a *New York Times* writer, his wife Lillian has "kept me goin'. She never lost faith, and that's a rare thing. I don't know now how we got through it, but we got through it."[10]

The story of Mac Sledge's conversion, like most of the other important events in the film, takes place off stage.[11] We see him in church where Rosa Lee is singing in the choir, "Jesus, Savior, Pilot Me." Sunny is baptized and the church sits in silence as Mac Sledge goes next. Someone says routinely, "Amen." As the family is driving home after church, Sunny says, "Well, we done it Mac, we were baptized. Everybody said I was gonna feel like a changed person. I guess I do feel a little different but not a whole lot different. Do you?"

Sledge shakes his head. No lightening bolt has struck him thus far. Sunny says, "You don't look any different," and Sledge smiles. "Not yet." As critic Pauline Kael remarked, "Mac's conversion, like his falling in love, takes place off camera; that could be one of the mercies referred to in the title."[12] Precisely! But in contrast to Kael's skepticism, this is perfectly congruent with the theme of faith in the hidden mercies of God, the secret plot of the life of faith in Romans. A few days later the scene shifts to a small dance hall where the new country band is performing. Sledge is singing a new song he had composed, about his beloved holding a ladder while he climbs up to the top. This expresses the plot of our text. Grace—someone else holding the ladder. And faith—climbing up when it is available. The ultimate source of the ladder in Mac Sledge's life may be invisible and off camera to him as well as to us, but he senses it is there and holds on tight to the future that has been given to him. To use the words from Paul once again, "For this [reason it is] from faith, thus according to grace" (Rom. 4:16).

At the end of the film, having attended his daughter's funeral after she was killed in a car accident, Sledge is picking up junk at the edge of the road near the house. Sunny comes home from school and asks his mother how his father was killed in Vietnam. She replies that it could have been a battle, or he could have been out walking. No one knows. Sunny goes outdoors with his football and runs toward Sledge. They throw the ball back and forth while Rosa Lee looks on from the house. A new future is emerging between a stepfather and his son, slowly and unexpectedly in the midst of the mysteries of life and death. The message of this film is that we have no final assurances, any more than Abraham did. But we can respond in faith to the tender mercies we have received.

The Structure of Divine Reversal

Paul describes the structure of these tender mercies in a way that is rather congruent with the film. He uses two succinct clauses in Rom 4:17 to describe the God of mercies, the One in whom Abraham "had faith,"

1) "who gives life to the dead"
2) "and calls that which does not exist into being"

While the concepts of resurrection and creation come from Paul's Jewish tradition,[13] his formulation suggests a parallel structure to salvation by faith, to resurrection from the dead, and to creation from nothing. As Käsemann explains, "creation, resurrection and justification declare in fact one and the same divine action. This means that justification, as the restitution of creation . . . is the decisive motif of Paul's soteriology."[14] Abraham was saved by faith, but the gift of a future to him did not depend on his prior achievement or virtue. The promise was given to him as a sheer gift, unearned and undeserved. Paul perceived the same structure in the theme of resurrection. The God who "gives life to the dead"[15] provides a future for those who have lost everything, even life itself. The dead have no power to save themselves. Resurrection, the central theme of Easter faith, is God's miraculous intervention in behalf of those who are powerless, whose time is up. But Paul finds the same structure in the symbol of creation itself. God "calls that which does not exist into being." The Creator-God always makes something out of nothing, expressing transcendence over the created order and freedom from cultural manipulation.[16]

A structure of divine reversal thus stands at the heart of the Abrahamic faith in the mercies of God. Those who deserve no mercy receive it; those who are dead are offered new life; and that which is nothing is brought into existence. This structure lies at the heart of every authentic experience of tender mercies, including Horton Foote's story. That Mac Sledge does not deserve the mercies of God is honestly portrayed throughout the film. He is a profane, bitter, destructive person at the very end of his resources. One of the saddest scenes in the film is when his daughter Sue Ann comes to visit. Sledge indicates he had written letters over the years, but she never got them. Her mother had tried to cut off all relationship with her destructive former husband. "I told mamma I was coming," Sue Ann confided. "She said she'd have me arrested if I did." Finally in this awkward and tentative scene Sue Ann asks about the song about the dove he had sung to her when she was young, about the "wings of a white dove." Sledge says "No . . . maybe it was someone else." Film critic Colin Westerbeck writes, "This exchange seems to be just the last of many missteps in their reunion, a final and rather minor failure of memory to make up for absence."[17] But I think Horton Foote had something much more significant in mind. This is a denial of a decent and tenderly caring aspect of Sledge's relationship to his daughter years ago. His singing had conveyed a sense of divine care that the child had needed and now yearns for again, far more than the fancy cars and big allowances that her mother was providing.

> On the wings of a snow white dove,
>> He came with his pure white love,
> With light from above,
>> On the wings of a dove.

Mac Sledge had conveyed God's tender mercy to his daughter without fully understanding it himself, and now he turns his back on it. Only when his daughter drives off—for the last time before her fatal automobile accident—does he return to the living room humming the song he knows full well. It is a failure that he will never be able to redress.

This theme of personal, moral, and spiritual failure is closely linked with the death and resurrection theme in the film. That Sledge for all effects and purposes was dead at the beginning of the film is strongly suggested by the photography. His consciousness of the threat of death is also conveyed by curious details in the dialogue. When he can't sing one of the songs he has written because his voice is shot, he says with irritation, "Don't feel sorry for me, Rosa Lee, I'm not dead yet." Later he is asked by a fan of the new band that is playing his music, "Hey mister, were you really Mac Sledge?" He smiles and says, "I guess I was." But it is in reaction to the accident involving his daughter that Sledge confronts the reality and puzzle of death most directly. He tells Rosa Lee about how he might well have died in place of his daughter:

> I was almost killed once in a car accident . . . I was drunk. They took me out of the car for dead, but I lived. I prayed last night to know why I lived and she died. But I got no answer to my prayer. I still don't know why she died and I lived. I don't know a blessed thing. I don't know why I came back to this part of Texas, and you took me in and straightened me out. Why, why did that happen? Is there a reason? And Sunny's daddy died in the war. My daughter killed in an automobile accident. Why? See, I don't trust happiness.

Mac Sledge can't trust happiness because it remains inexplicable. But he does trust the tender mercies that mysteriously led him from death to life. But it is also a leading from nothingness to existence, to use the words of Romans.

Sledge is depicted as having nothing at the start of the story. He has lost his voice and his talent along with his future. His career is gone. His family is gone. As a schoolboy taunted Sunny in the playground, the man staying at their home is nothing but a "silly drunk." And yet mysteriously in the course of the film, Sledge begins to be someone again. He gradually regains the use of his talents. As a film reviewer remarked, Sledge "is, like the legendary Phoenix, to rise from the ashes."[18] Although low-key throughout, this story tells of something just as miraculous as the creation of something out of nothing celebrated by biblical writers. Another reviewer describes the filmmaker's intent: "Bent on celebrating the recuperative power of the human spirit, he leads his hero into temptation but delivers him from evil, and the audience I was in seemed dazed by the euphoria of witnessing a miracle."[19] But unlike the usual miracles of film and television fantasy, this one occurs mysteriously, off camera. That's what dazes us. It is a matter of faith, elusive and intangible. All we can witness is that a person who was once almost nothing becomes something at the end of the story, singing his own new songs and tossing a football to his newfound son.

Holding Fast to Elusive Mercy

God's mercy appears most often beyond the range of the camera. The Creator does not ordinarily come out into the open as in the film *Oh, God!* in which he takes the form of a determined George Burns who performs public miracles to convince the world of his message. These two films, in fact, embody opposing strands in our religious heritage. In *Oh, God!* we find the pseudo-scientific notion that God demonstrates his existence by performing miracles out in the open. When an automobile is filled with water on command right in the middle of the street on a dry day as in *Oh, God!* a definitiveness typical of Fundamentalism is being claimed in the proof of God's existence and power.[20] But

Horton Foote's script is closer to the biblical truth. God's ways are too elusive[21] for science, too far off the graph for objective proof. Yet the miracles of mercy are there for all who have faith to see.

So the final question is this: can Americans, who prefer pragmatic evidence, learn to gaze beneath the surface of their lives to discern the hidden plot of tender mercies? Can they develop the skill and courage to follow the tiny clues that may lead to a viable future, despite failures and betrayals? The work of Horton Foote and the apostle Paul suggests a holding fast to the mercies received, no matter how far off stage they may be occurring. It calls for faith in the God of tender mercies, for faithfulness to the relationships through which those mercies are conveyed. Despite the need to maintain a scientific outlook, there is no need to repudiate the simple ways of conveying God's "pure sweet love" to other people, "on the wings of a dove." For the God of tender mercies is the final source of any knowledge we may have into the mystery of life. The God of Abraham and Sarah and Paul is the one "who gives life to the dead and calls that which does not exist into being" . . . even in America!

6

Righteous Gentiles
in *Grand Canyon*

For it is not the hearers of the law who are righteous before God,
but the doers of the law who shall be made right.
For when the Gentiles that do not have the law do by nature
the things of the law, they are a law even though they themselves do not have the law. Such people demonstrate that the
works of the law are written in their hearts, their conscience
also confirming, and the conflicting thoughts condemning or
apologizing, [and they shall be made right] on the day when
God judges the secrets of humans through Christ Jesus, according to my gospel.

(Rom. 2:13–16)

But we know that for those who love God,
    all things work together for good;
        for those who are called according to God's purpose,
because those whom she foreknew,
    she also predestined to be conformed to the image of her son,
        in order that he might be the firstborn of many brothers
        [and sisters];
and those whom God predestined he also called;
    and those whom he called, he also made right;
        and those God made right, she also glorified.[1]

(Rom. 8:28–30)

Paul's description of Gentiles who "do by nature the things of the law" was embodied in an impressive recent film. *Grand Canyon* [2] tells the story of people who seem to have the "law written in their hearts." Simon, a black tow truck driver in Los Angeles, risks his life to rescue a motorist, Mac, who is imperiled by robbers. They and their families subsequently become friends who discover the "miracles" of everyday life. Claire, the wife of the white lawyer rescued by Simon, shows herself to be a righteous Gentile when she finds an abandoned infant and convinces her husband that they should carry through with adoption. The themes in this film resonate with several passages in Paul's letter to the Romans dealing with the righteous Gentiles and divine providence. But film critic David Anson calls *Grand Canyon* "the season's most fascinating failure" because its "vague cosmic notions of the 'miracles of daily life' can't see us through the current troubles in the city."[3]

Is Paul's idea of righteous Gentiles a chimera? Can we believe that the miracles of everyday experience point toward a predestined plan of God? Is such providence capable of seeing us through our current troubles? These questions gain significance from the fact that the story of *Grand Canyon* takes place in the same portion of Los Angeles that was destroyed by the riots in May, 1992. As Danny Glover said in a televised interview about his role of Simon in this film, the movie was "prophetic."

The Puzzling Theme of Righteous Gentiles

The idea of righteous Gentiles, of pagans who do what the law requires even though they never read the Bible, is a controversial part of Romans. At first glance Paul's argument that "it is . . . the doers of the law who shall be made right," or as in most translations, "shall be justified," seems to contradict the central thesis of his letter. If all humans are sinners (Rom. 3:9, 23) and if no one can be "justified by works of the law" (Rom. 3:20), how can Paul suggest here that there are some people who "do by nature the things of the law" (2:14)?

A recent study by Klyne Snodgrass[4] has addressed these questions in a manner that opens a way to consider the affinity with *Grand Canyon*. When Paul refers to "works" and "what the law requires" in Romans 2, he has in mind persons "who live obediently in accordance with the revelation they have received."[5] They meet the needs of others without self-serving motives, and thus fulfill the law's requirement of integrity. By contrast, when Paul refers to "works of the law" being unable to provide salvation in 3:20, he has in mind the "works righteousness" by which people conform to the law in order to gain status.[6]

It is this kind of perverse motivation that appears to be absent from Simon and Claire. They repudiate manipulation and do not feel the need to be thanked for what they have done. For instance, Claire explains to her husband that her motivation for adopting the child she had found was not a matter of filling some kind of "hole in my life. . . . That baby needs someone to love it and take care of it." She simply responds to the law written on her heart, responding to the baby's need for care.

The presence of the law written on the heart is also confirmed, as far as Paul is concerned, by internal moral accountability. He refers to Gentiles having a "conscience . . . [that] bears witness" and to "conflicting thoughts" that accuse or excuse them (Rom. 2:15). When people display this kind of accountability, it is evidence that they genuinely are human.[7] This trait of moral responsibility is impressively displayed both in Simon and in Claire. When Simon reasons with the gang leader who wants to steal Mac's stalled car, he says: "Now this truck is my responsibility. Now that the car is hooked up to it, I'm responsible for that too. . . . I got to get out of here, and you got the gun. So I am asking you for a favor to let us out of here." Though Simon grapples with moral dilemmas and sometimes doesn't know what to do, he acts responsibly in caring for his sister's family, which is surviving in the ghetto without a father. He is equally responsible in communicating with his daughter, who is in a school for the deaf in Washington. Claire also is caught in moral conflicts and is deeply puzzled about what life is about, yet she is shown to be responsible in her use of time, in her care for her son and husband, and in caring for the infant she found.

To have the law written on the heart and to do instinctively what the law requires does not imply making perfect decisions. Snodgrass points out that the argument in Romans 2:1–16 and 25–29 is that salvation and damnation are a result of one's actions, taking into consideration the amount of revelation given."[8] Paul does not imply that righteous Gentiles always and in every instance respond perfectly to the law written on the heart. Similarly in *Grand Canyon*, neither Simon nor Claire is depicted as perfect. He has a failed marriage behind him and is overly cynical at times about the goodness of life. Claire is shown to be a little obsessive in her work with voluntary organizations, keeping her calendar overly straight. There is no hint of an explicitly religious background in either of them. But when these "righteous Gentiles" encounter someone they can help, they rise to the occasion.

One reason Paul can acknowledge virtue in persons far beyond the boundaries of any chosen people is his assumption that salvation through Christ brings humans into contact with the same "gracious, acting God" who has sustained life throughout the world before and after the Christ event.[9] God acts outside as well as inside of faith communities. I believe this is a crucial assumption as far as Paul's argument in Romans is concerned, because the letter as a whole aims at a missionary goal. Paul writes to elicit support for the mission to the pagans in Spain.[10]

This theme resonates with the secular arena of the film: miracles occur here outside the church. Yet the source of righteousness in these contemporary Gentiles is also visible, despite the limited horizons of the film. In the first conversation after bringing Mac's car back safely into the service station, Simon describes his central premise:

> Man, get yourself to the Grand Canyon. . . . Those cliffs and rocks are so old. . . . When you sit on the edge of that thing you just realize what a joke we people are, the big heads we got that all we do is going to matter all that much, thinking our time here makes a difference to those rocks. . . . When you sit on the edge of that thing—I felt like a gnat that lands on the ass of a cow that's chewing its cud next to a road that you ride by at seventy miles an hour. . . . You're small, you're small.

Simon's reflections on the vast canyon bring him to insights similar to those Paul refers to in Romans 1:20, that every person has access to God's "eternal power and divinity, invisible though they are," because they can be perceived in the "creation of the world." To acknowledge this is to avoid the idolatry described in Romans 1, and to remain capable of responsible behavior. In the end, Simon helps the other persons in the story to understand the meaning of the Grand Canyon for themselves.

Film critic Stanley Kauffmann finds it incomprehensible that the mere sight of the Grand Canyon could make Simon feel "minute and transitory. At the end, all of the principals visit the Grand Canyon together and, presumably, feel minute and transitory together. What this has to do with the immediate pressure of daily problems the film doesn't bother to reveal."[11] The connection is perfectly clear when we view this film through the eyes of Paul.

One of the most significant insights emerging out of recent research on Romans relates to the purpose of Paul's discussion of the righteous Gentiles. Paul's aim "is clearly to puncture a Jewish assurance falsely based on the fact of having the law, of being the chosen people of God," in the words of commentator James Dunn.[12] It therefore fits the thrust of the letter as a whole, which seeks to find common ground between competitive and hostile groups by shattering all illusions of cultural superiority.

This reaches to the heart of the attitudes that surfaced after *Grand Canyon* appeared. In the Simi Valley verdict on the policemen who beat Rodney King and the subsequent Los Angeles riots, it became clear that neither blacks nor whites, neither Hispanics nor Asians wish to give up their claims of moral superiority, to recognize there are righteous Gentiles in the other side. The matter of feeling superior was a crucial factor both in the verdict and in the ensuing riot, in which discriminatory actions by various ethnic groups in Los Angeles surfaced. The Simi Valley is populated largely by persons escaping the high-crime areas of the city, and thus a jury from there was inclined to favor the police over a black motorist. This was also a key factor in the "proactive" strategy of the Los Angeles police force under Superintendent Daryl Gates,[13] who viewed the ghetto public as the enemy requiring military means of coercion through SWAT teams and other forms of intimidation.[14] The menacing police helicopters in *Grand Canyon* convey this theme very well, as does the opening dialogue of the film about the citizenry being obsessed with "control, control, control" because they are all afraid of what the city might do to them. The premise of such fear is that there are no righteous Gentiles, that members of other racial groups are inherently dangerous. But the consequence of such a premise is undue brutality in dealing with others, which produces resentments that could blow a city apart at any time.

But there *are* righteous Gentiles out there, in various groups. Particularly memorable was the spontaneous intervention of four black citizens of East Los Angeles who witnessed the brutal beating and shooting of the white trucker Reginald Denny. They came to the scene as quickly as they could, drew him back into his vehicle, and drove him to the hospital, probably saving his life. It was a real-life enactment of the story of *Grand Canyon*, confirming the truth and relevance of the Pauline hope. And like Simon and Claire in the film, none of them seemed particularly interested in touting their heroism in interviews after the riot. They had done what seemed natural, because the law was written on their heart.

Shouldn't the presence of such persons help to soften attitudes toward other cultural groups in this country? Such softening might enable citizens to listen more closely to the law written on the heart, which would have a decisive effect on what Anson called "the current troubles in the city."

The Outworking of Providence

This leads to the theme of providence that is central to the story of *Grand Canyon*. In Romans 8 Paul claims that "all things work together for good for those who are called according to his purpose." That things will work out for the best was "a common axiom of antiquity" in the Greco-Roman world,[15] but as Dunn has shown, Paul probably has in mind the Jewish theme of divine providence.[16] Behind the mixture of good and evil in present-day experience, divine providence is at work, drawing events toward a good end. This fits one of Claire's lines in the film: "Everything seems so close together . . . all the good and bad things."[17] The idea that something good comes out of this mixture is a miracle that touches everyone in the film, one way or another. The good and bad events in the film are understood to be the outworking of a mysterious, miracle-working power, bringing people together and revealing their destinies in one another.

The full scope of predestination as explained by Paul is not in view, because no one in the film comes to what Christian theologians might accept as an adequate grasp of his or her destiny. But the optimistic outcome of the story is captured by the wording of Romans 8:28, that everything, the tragic as well as the good, works "together for good." It is a remarkably open formulation, pertaining to believers and nonbelievers alike. God is truly at work everywhere. In this sense the film broadens the theme of predestination in the same generous direction promoted by Romans. But the fallen world remains a reality, providing the context of the "all things" that happen to humans, both good and ill. It is a world thoroughly corrupted by sin. As Simon tells the thugs, "this is not the way it was meant to be." But this is the way it is in Los Angeles and elsewhere, where crime and violent coercion mark our culture.

Paul does not claim this providential outworking will automatically be fulfilled for everyone. He specifies in Romans that "all things work together for good . . . for those who are called according to God's purpose." He then goes on to refer to God's calling, which, if one responds to it, will lead to people being set right or "justified" and even, in the end, "glorified." This is an impressive theme in the film. After Mac is rescued by Simon, he gets a strong sense that he should respond to the relationship, even though lawyers ordinarily do not become close friends with truck drivers, or blacks with whites. He invites Simon out for breakfast and in the conversation relates an incident that had occurred on the "Miracle Mile" of Wilshire Boulevard when a strange hand held him back from stepping into the street in front of a speeding bus. He had thanked the woman, who was oddly dressed in a Pittsburgh Pirates baseball hat, his own favorite team, but she got away and he never saw her again. "I never got over the idea that I should have talked to that woman more," he tells Simon. So Mac persists in responding to this strange sense of calling to do better with Simon.

Claire also develops a strong sense that there was a reason she found the baby in the bushes. She explains her conviction to Mac that finding the child was similar to Simon saving Mac in the ghetto. "Something has happened. . . . Some kind of connection has been made and it has to be played out. . . . What if these are miracles, Mac. Maybe we don't have any experience with miracles, so we're slow to recognize them." Mac replies that he has a headache, but she rejects that response as inappropriate in the face of a miracle. Just as in Romans, it is necessary for people to recognize and hold fast to the providential purpose that is opening up for them. Otherwise, it can be lost.

Laying Hold of Providence

In *Grand Canyon*, it is the Hollywood producer Davis who comes to embody the theme of refusing providence. He experienced the kind of random violence he had loved to film when a mugger shot him in the thigh because he didn't turn over his Rolex as quickly and politely as he might have. While in the hospital, he had what he called a "vision," which could have led him to abandon the irresponsible way he was living. Later he explained to Claire "what was delivered unto me" in the vision, reverting to pious, biblical language for the first time in the film. She smiled at the "unto" language that sounded so strange for this cynical friend, but he insisted it was "a religious experience." The message of this vision was that he should not make another movie that "glorifies violence and bloodshed and brutality. I can't contribute another stone to this landslide of dehumanizing rage that swept across this country like a pestilence. . . . No more exploding bodies. . . . I'm going to make the world a better place for your new bambino." Given the significant problem with violence in American media, emphasized by repeated glimpses of brutal conflict on television screens throughout *Grand Canyon*, this resolve is admirable. Davis also takes up a more responsible relationship with his girlfriend.

Eventually, however, Davis turns away from this calling to become a more responsible filmmaker, saying, "I must have been delirious" to have had that vision in the hospital. He goes back to making violent films, explaining the vast gulf that is opening in this country between people who have something and others who have nothing. It's as big as the Grand Canyon, and out of this abyss comes "an eruption of rage, and rage creates violence and the violence is real . . . and nothing's going to make it go away. Until someone changes something, which is not going to happen. . . . With so much rage going around, we're damn lucky we have the movies to help us vent a little of it." Mac says he is surprised that Davis would use this tired line about venting rage through depicting it. This theory has repeatedly been disproven by studies that indicate cinematic violence tends to desensitize people so they become more prone to violent behavior themselves. But Davis would not be impressed by such arguments. He refers to an old movie that Mac had not seen about a man who had lost sight of what he was on this earth to do. "Fortunately he finds his way back." He thinks Mac should do the same, but the audience knows that Davis is the one who should find what he is on earth to do.

The film thus confronts Americans with a choice between two Grand Canyons. The one is the Grand Canyon of rage, to which each is inclined at times to contribute. It is the abyss that opened in one of the greatest American cities in May of 1992. And it could do so for every community, every institution, every church in this country. The other Grand Canyon is formed by divine providence, which could lead the country through difficult times to a more promising future. It is the same choice that Paul poses in Romans. Will people respond to the odd experiences that call them according to God's purpose? Will they turn away from destructive forms of behavior that may appear to bring success, but which actually ruin the city?

In the words of Romans 2:13 will America become, like Davis, a mere hearer of the law, rather than a doer of the law? Both in the experience of providence in individual lives, and in the words of the law, there is a call to responsibility. The typical American privatization of salvation is sadly manifest in the film: Davis does accept a kind of marital responsibility but refuses to change his approach to his vocation. He continues to celebrate the fall into violence, the false Grand Canyon of rage.

The Climax of Reflected Glory

Fortunately neither the film nor Paul suggests that this kind of impasse is inevitable. In Romans 8, Paul offers the magnificent climax that leads from "calling" to divine foreknowledge, to "predestined," to being "made right," and finally to being "glorified." *Grand Canyon* picks up this theme of glory and makes a significant religious statement, despite its flaws, its brutal images, its crude language, and its occasional shallowness. The final scene depicts both families led by their righteous Gentiles piling out of a van at the edge of the Grand Canyon. Several of them have responded faithfully to their new calling and are becoming righteous. Claire and Mac have adopted the baby. Simon's new girlfriend is there, after the miracle of their blind date arranged by Mac. Even Mac's and Claire's son, Roberto, is along, despite the fact that he is now fifteen and ordinarily would not be expected to take a trip with his parents, especially without his girlfriend.

Simon's alienated nephew gets out of the van with irritation on his face, but then changes as he sees a glimmer of transcendence at the sight of the tremendous canyon. Now he may catch a glimpse of the meaning of his life, so that the fear he has of not surviving as a black youth until the age of twenty-five may pass away in the broader vista of the canyon. The camera allows us to see this remarkable scene of black and white families, standing side by side at the edge of the canyon, embodying the true solidarity of the "many brethren" referred to in Romans 8. There is a wonderful sense of reflected glory as this group of new friends stands alongside the magnificent canyon. They gaze in awe at the grandest symbol of transcendence in North America, and the camera moves out over the canyon to capture their glowing faces, standing side by side, black and white, caught by rapture. They are beautiful, each one, reflecting a bit of that glory of the "children of God," yearning for freedom from bondage to violence and futility.

Those "whom God made right, God also glorified" (Rom. 8:30). It is a destiny that Paul would desire for every person in the story, so the troubled city itself might one day be set right.

7

Tootsie and
the Comfort of Christ

Blessed be the God and Father of our Lord Jesus Christ,
    the Father of mercies
        and God of all comfort,
who comforts us in all our affliction,
    so that we may be able to comfort those who are in
    any affliction,
        through the comfort with which we ourselves are
        comforted by God.
For as we abound in Christ's sufferings,
    so through Christ we abound in comfort too.
If we are afflicted,
    it is for your comfort and salvation;
and if we are comforted,
    it is for your comfort,
        which you experience when you patiently endure the
        same sufferings that we suffer.
Our hope for you is also unshaken;
    for we know that as you share in our sufferings,
        you also share in our comfort.

                        (2 Cor. 1:3–7)

Some time ago I was asked to speak in a program sponsored by the Women's Images Center at Garrett-Evangelical Theological Seminary on the matter of male and female identities. I found myself thinking of *Tootsie*,[1] whose story resonates with the theme of comfort in the text from 2 Corinthians. The most widely quoted line in the film comes when Michael is explaining himself to Julie, who has just discovered that he had been impersonating an actress when he became her closest friend in the cast of a soap opera. Here are the words that Dustin Hoffman said as Michael: "I was a better man with you as a woman than I ever was with a woman as a man."

The idea of being able to comfort others because of sharing their situation is what connects *Tootsie* with its improbable-sounding counterpart in 2 Corinthians. The film reveals that playing other people's roles and facing the afflictions they face has a humanizing effect. It allows relations without pretensions or concerns about superiority. People can say to each other, I know a little about how you feel, because I walked a ways in those same mocassins. Or as Paul stated it, we are "able to comfort those who are in any affliction through the comfort with which we ourselves are comforted by God" (2 Cor. 1:4). In this verse the major themes in the opening section of 2 Corinthians are stated: affliction, comfort, and the strange proportionality between the two. Each theme is embodied in the film *Tootsie*.

Forms of Affliction

Paul's discussion of the comfort of Christ came after the resolution of one of the worst conflicts in his checkered career. It involved many of the factors experienced in the past years in many Christian communities in the United States—tensions between sexes, races, and classes. In Corinth it also involved broken relationships in which the memory of things said in anger still lingered. There were false expectations and broken promises that caused bitter feelings.

Intentional and unintentional betrayals had produced a trail of mutual accusations. Conflicts over leadership and strategy were threatening the unity and mission of the church.

Paul uses one word for all such troubles: *thlipsis*, "affliction, or trouble." "Blessed be the God and Father of our Lord Jesus Christ . . . who comforts us in all our affliction, so that we may be able to comfort those who are in any affliction" (2 Cor. 1:3–4). To understand the relevance of these words, we need to reconstruct the troubles that Paul and the Corinthians had suffered. It is clear that traveling Christian evangelists had come to Corinth in Paul's absence. They arrived in the middle of a church conflict involving at least four factions that are mentioned in 1 Corinthians 1–3. Calling themselves "superapostles," they carried letters of recommendation from churches where they had been successful. With great eloquence and personal charisma, they initiated a systematic attack on Paul's theology and leadership.

The superapostles charged that Paul was an inferior apostle, because he was disaster prone. He had a miserable record of having trouble with the authorities, provoking riots, and being flogged in synagogues. He was forced to earn his living as a menial tentmaker. These attacks were part of a larger theological and ecclesiastical program. In the words of Corinthians commentator Victor Furnish, the invading missionaries supported their claims of superiority "not only by letters of recommendation, pretentiously boasting about their being of Jewish stock and about special 'signs' of their apostleship: their rhetorical eloquence and impressive personal bearing, their boldness and missionary achievements, their ecstatic experiences, their special religious knowledge derived from extraordinary visions and revelations, and their ability to perform miracles."[2] The superapostles had a kind of macho image of Christ and themselves and a superheroic, success-oriented theology to match.[3] They taught that a true Christian never experiences affliction. These preachers were smooth, well educated, and eloquent speakers, and their message of super-Christianity swept the divided Corinthian congregation off its feet. How could they resist the idea that their charismatic gifts, leadership abilities, and intelligence should not promise power, success, and wealth? Why shouldn't they enjoy a superior status in comparison with Paul and others who were experiencing afflictions?

The appeal of the superapostles was a little like Michael and his playwright roommate holding circles of young Thespians spellbound at the beginning of *Tootsie*. They maintained the pretension of knowing all the angles, of having mastered the route that theater people have to travel to success in New York. They were somewhat older than their admiring listeners, worldly wise, and spouting all the right formulas. The film reveals the hollowness of this pose of superiority, because in fact both Michael and his roommate are failures whose pretensions have virtually ruined their careers. But their stance of superiority keeps them from seeing this. Like the overbearing superapostles in Corinth, they are able to convince gullible listeners as well.

The wonderful thing about the film is that the audience can see itself so clearly in the story. How many times have men or women taken the superior line with each other? How instinctively whites take it upon themselves to give the wise word to blacks or Native Americans, and how often do they claim to possess the superior insight for others as well? At least some of the afflictions experienced recently by Americans are caused in part by hollow rhetoric that feigns super status.

The affliction that Paul speaks of in 2 Corinthians also includes elements of betrayal. It is evident from the way Paul apologizes for his changed travel plans in chapter 1, for instance, that the congregation feels he had broken his word. He reiterates his original plans "to visit you on my way to Macedonia and to come back to you from Macedonia and have you send me on my way to Judea" (2 Cor. 1:16). But then he is forced to explain why he decided to change these plans: "it was to spare you that I refrained from coming to Corinth" (2 Cor. 1:23). The succeeding verses reveal that the Corinthians charged Paul with "vacillating." In contrast to the superapostles, who allegedly always kept their appointments, Paul is accused of being unable to make up his mind. He said he would do one thing and then stood them up, which fit right in with the charges the superapostles were making. Paul is a false apostle, they claimed. He has acted "according to worldly standards"[4] in breaking his commitment to arrive in Corinth.

The experience of affliction also included Paul's sense of having been betrayed by the Corinthians. He referred to the visit he recently had made to Corinth, a visit so "painful" (2 Cor. 2:1) that he decided not to repeat it, no matter what travel plans he had made with the Corinthians. As scholars piece the story together, it seems that Paul had tried to cope with the superapostle threat in person, only to have the congregation line up against him. He left Corinth in defeat, repudiated by the very persons his gospel had redeemed. As Furnish reconstructs the situation, "Paul's unplanned, emergency visit to Corinth had been a disaster. He must have hurried back to Ephesus hurt, angered, and perplexed."[5] He was humiliated, tearful, and furious that the congregation he had served could have accepted the success-oriented nonsense of fraudulent apostles whose aim was to exploit the church for their own profit.

Betrayal is also central to *Tootsie*. After Michael gets the soap opera job playing the role of a matronly hospital administrator, his double life causes one betrayal after the next. He stands up his girlfriend Sandy time after time. He arrives at ten thirty for a seven o'clock dinner invitation. He is never in the apartment when he is supposed to be to take her calls. While planning to be with her in a play project, Michael falls in love with Julie, the romantic lead in the soap program. But there is an element of betrayal in this as well, since Julie thinks of him as Dorothy, a mentor with whom she could share intimate details that she would never entrust to a man. These betrayals all cause pain, which the fantasy world of film allows to be resolved by happy endings. Since such resolutions rarely occur in real life, film critic Vincent Canby observes that this film "makes plausibility look obsolete."[6]

The matter of betrayal is something many of us have experienced in religious institutions in recent years when worthy causes have multiplied and organizational energies and resources have diminished. Some leaders have organized protests that others have criticized, or arranged services and programs that their friends failed to support or attend. Many sincere members of religious organizations have been forced to take sides or perhaps were too committed to other causes to undertake new obligations, with the result that others felt betrayed. As I look back over the past several years in the volatile atmosphere of a controversial theological seminary, I find myself regretting some intemperate words and wishing I had consulted with colleagues more faithfully. Perhaps other persons in similar situations feel the same way. It seems that no matter what role one plays in the give and take of Christian communities, betrayal is part of affliction.

The final form of affliction in 2 Corinthians has to do with separation. Paul was agonized by the distance between himself and the congregation. Communications by letter and messenger were slow, infrequent, and unreliable. Paul was caught in a network of other obligations. He had other churches to deal with, each with problems of its own. He was operating under severe economic constraints, having to put in twelve-hour days as a handworker simply to earn food and lodging.[7] In addition to these troubles that kept him from returning to Corinth, he had suffered during this period a humiliating and life-threatening imprisonment, the so-called "affliction in Asia."[8]

These trials sound familiar for many members of our congregations and of our clergy in these days of economic and emotional insecurity. Adverse economic conditions are affecting the farming and manufacturing communities across the country. Budgets of religious institutions and governmental agencies have repeatedly been cut. Branches of the church are threatening the role of independent scholarship in colleges and seminaries. In other quarters there are campaigns to suppress leadership of women. The list of threatening circumstances could be enlarged considerably.

In Paul's case there was the added burden of the broken relationship with the Corinthians. He describes the crippling effect of these emotional scars in 2 Cor. 2:12–13: "When I came to Troas on behalf of the gospel of Christ, a door having been opened for me in the Lord, my anxiety was unrelieved because I did not find my brother Titus there."[9] With Titus not arriving with good news from Corinth, Paul was too upset to work effectively. He traveled on to Macedonia, in the hope of meeting Titus halfway. Later in the letter, Paul describes his troubled mind just before Titus arrived with the good news that the Corinthians were reconciled: "For even when we came into Macedonia, our bodies had no rest but we were afflicted at every turn—fighting without and fear within. But God, who comforts the downcast, comforted us by the coming of Titus, and not only by his coming but also by the comfort with which he was comforted in you" (2 Cor. 7:5–7).

The agonies of separation that Paul experienced were matched to some degree in *Tootsie*. In addition to the economic and temperamental problems that Michael and his friends confront, there was the effect of sexual stereotypes. In the course of the film, Michael's ploy to get out of the unemployment lines by impersonating a soap opera actress led him to discover the alienation of second-class citizenship. He decides to ask his agent to get him other female roles, but George finds it laughable that Michael would have anything significant to say to women. "I have plenty to say to women," Mike argues. "I've been an unemployed actor for twenty years, George. I know what it's like to sit by the phone waiting for it to ring. And when I finally get a job, I have no control. Everybody else has the power and I got zip." Not only has Michael learned something about the status of women; he has also developed a deeper understanding of his own humanity. In this sense, *Tootsie* makes a valuable contribution to our understanding of the relations between men and women in a liberated era. As Declan Kiberd showed in his survey *Men and Feminism in Modern Literature*, "Women might become honorary men . . . but few men were prepared to become honorary women. . . . At the root of the defiant masculinity of the majority lay the fear of feminisation and of lost power."[10] In this movie, we see an unexpected possibility, that a new and more honest self-image can arise in a rather arrogant male as a result of experiencing the afflictions that women routinely face: separation, powerlessness, lower pay, and low esteem.[11] For the first time, Michael was rendered capable of experiencing what Paul called "comfort."

The Correlation Between Affliction and Comfort

The comfort that Paul describes in 2 Corinthians was a matter of experiencing solidarity with other people, but in a context that is not fully matched in a film like *Tootsie*. This peculiar context is "the comfort of Christ." Paul believed that Christ shares human affliction to an ultimate degree. He died a human death. He not only took the afflictions deserved by others upon himself but even received the betrayals and denials of his most courageous disciples. When believers discover the depth of divine love for them, they are in Paul's words, "comforted by God. For as we abound in Christ's sufferings, so through Christ we abound in comfort too" (2 Cor. 1:4–5).

The comfort of Christ provides Paul with the moral courage needed to work for genuine reconciliation. It is worth observing that such comfort did not lead Paul to drop the struggle for honesty. He refused to let the congregation get away with a cheap betrayal of their relationship to him, to live within a network of lies about themselves and the superapostles. Paul writes letters and makes painful visits to straighten things out. He does not give up until reconciliation is genuine. There is an allusion to the painful price of such honesty in verse 6 of our text: "If we are afflicted, it is for your comfort and salvation; and if we are comforted, it is for your comfort, which you experience when you patiently endure the same sufferings that we suffer."

One of the appealing aspects of the character Dorothy that Michael impersonates in the film is her courage to insist on decency. She refuses the demeaning nickname "Tootsie," which the television director Ron likes to use for subordinate females. And she sustains her new friend, Julie (played by Jessica Lange), who needs to make a break from an abusive relationship with Ron. On the night when Julie makes up her mind to take that step, she refers to the fact that Dorothy has been a good influence.

> "Why shouldn't you influence me?" Julie asks. "Listen, you wouldn't compromise your feelings like I have. You wouldn't live this kind of life, would you?"
>
> "Well, no, I wouldn't, but . . ." Dorothy replies.
>
> "Of course not, and you're right," says Julie. "I deserve something better, you know. I don't have to settle for this. It's just that I've always been too lazy, or too scared. . . . I'll live, maybe not happily, but honestly. Hm. Sounds like something you'd say!"

Genuine comfort is not cheap. It is not possible to find it when basic relationships remain dishonest. There is in fact a kind of equation, a proportionality, between honesty and genuine comfort. Without the one, it is impossible to sustain the other. That is part of the truth we discern as we reflect on *Tootsie* in the light of the comfort of Christ. Many are discovering the same thing as American congregations of the late twentieth century try to live out the gospel in pluralistic communities of men and women, blacks and whites, Latinos and Orientals.

But even more important, there is the substance of comfort itself. In Paul's case, it came in the form of the news that his colleague Titus brought concerning the reconciliation with the Corinthians. For Paul, this and all other forms of conflict resolution constitute the "comfort of Christ." The love of Christ sustains him through dark times, giving the courage to love his enemies and not to give up on his friends. That same divine love is at work in others, leading to growth and responsibility as the Corinthians finally see through the shallow gospel of the superapostles.

Paul's contention is that there is a profound correlation between affliction and comfort in Christ. It is only as people bear the suffering of Christ that they can experience the depth of the comfort of Christ.[12] Paul was convinced that God makes use of suffering, whatever its causes. Afflictions can destroy false claims of self-sufficiency as well as guises of superiority. When one faces an incurable illness, or a pain that no physician can relieve, or a misunderstanding that centuries of prejudice have caused, it becomes clear that no human being has all the answers. Everyone is vulnerable, limited, and fragmented. Because of our cultural legacy of sexual exploitation, domination, and role definitions, each man threatens the integrity of each woman, without even realizing it, just by doing what seems to come naturally. And each woman threatens the morale of each man, in opposite and correlative ways.

The presence of culturally shaped vulnerabilities made the superapostles in Corinth particularly dangerous for mature faith. They denied the reality of the human condition. They pretended to be self-sufficient, invulnerable, victorious, and at the same time, perfectly innocent. They denied their own motivations and fed themselves and their followers the most dangerous message of all: that faith makes people superior, changing them into superheroes who are invulnerable and unerring, never to be defeated by any odds.

For Paul, this superheroic gospel was a violation of the single most important reality in the Christian faith—that Christ died for all. Christ made himself as vulnerable as all humans in fact are. He refused to come down from the cross. So whatever people experience, whatever disappointment, betrayal, or death they suffer, they can be sure of one thing: Christ is with them, sharing every humiliation.

Comfort Without Happy Endings

Genuine faith in Christ crucified has a depth far beyond anything touched on in a film like *Tootsie*, because it provides the power to comfort one another even without happy endings. In the closing scene in the film, when Julie and Michael are being reconciled, she says,

> "I miss Dorothy."
> Michael replies, "You don't have to. She's right here. Look, you don't know me from Adam. But I was a better man with you as a woman than I ever was with a woman as a man. You know what I mean? I've just got to learn to do it without a dress. . . . The hard part's over. We're already good friends."

There is a sense in which members of the Christian community are also called upon to wear one another's clothes at times, to share others' burdens and afflictions. But in the end, people need to "learn to do it," to be human to each other, without the costume. This is related to the remarkable invitation the men received to participate in the service organized by the Women's Center mentioned earlier. We were asked to wear dresses for an hour, so to speak. None of us had particular qualifications for this task; we were probably not much more or less chauvinistic than the other males in our culture. But what we discovered was that taking a woman's role for a moment did not erode our masculinity. Richard Blake makes a related point in his review of *Tootsie:*

"When the characters discover the opposite sexual pole in their own personalities, they become more fully human."[13]

Christian believers are not asked to deny their sexual identities. This is clearly implied in Paul's use of the term *sôma*, "body," for the whole person.[14] The peculiar vulnerabilities of males and females are intrinsic to humanity; they are transformed but never eliminated by redemption in Christ. In fact, as people understand one another's afflictions more accurately, they are enabled to become more genuinely male and female, knowing that Christ has died to accept them precisely as they are, with all their peculiarities and contradictions.

It follows that there is no need to console ourselves with Michael's silly hope that "the hard part is over." Actually, it is likely to get worse, if the signs of the times are to be heeded. The most effective comfort males and females have to offer each other in difficult times is that they continue to *be* comforted in their own afflictions. The greatest assets believers have for one another in the broader ministry of the church are their failures, vulnerabilities, and fears. As far as the clergy is concerned, this assessment is likely the very opposite of the traditional perspective. Many people attend seminary to gain final answers for other people's religious problems, the inspired approach to controversial social issues, or the invulnerable defense of the true faith. But they should discover that playing god with others is not genuinely redemptive, either for themselves or for others. In the end everyone needs to discover what Paul finally grasped for himself in the aftermath of the Corinthian trauma: to heal other people requires the admission of one's own woundedness; no one can comfort others without acknowledging one's own need for comfort. In the words of Henri Nouwen, "Making one's own wounds a source of healing" involves "a constant willingness to see one's own pain and suffering as rising from the depth of the human condition which all men share."[15] This is also why the shared meal at the Lord's Table is so crucial for the health of

Christian disciples: those who are broken and sinful and thoughtless and arrogant need to participate frequently in the bread broken for them, in the blood that was shed for their redemption. "For as we abound in Christ's suffering, so through Christ we abound in comfort too" (2 Cor. 1:5).

8

Earthen Vessels
and *Ordinary People*

But we have this treasure in earthen vessels,
>   to show the transcendent power belongs to God and not
>   to ourselves.
>>   We are hard pressed in every way,
>>>   but not crushed;
>>   thrown into perplexity,
>>>   but not driven to despair;
>>   harassed,
>>>   but not abandoned;
>>   knocked down,
>>>   but not knocked out.
>   We always bear in our body the dying of Jesus,
>>   so that the life of Jesus may be displayed in our body.[1]

>>>>>>>>>>>>>>>>>>>>>>> (2 Cor. 4:7–10)

There is a classic novel by Judith Guest[2] that grapples with the pervasive American issue of perfectionism. To use words from Paul's discussion of the same issue in 2 Corinthians, *Ordinary People* deals with the impact of being knocked down, harassed, perplexed, and hard pressed. In the Academy Award–winning filming of this story,[3] Mary Tyler Moore plays Beth, the perfectionist mother who leaves her family because they remind her too painfully of her son's attempted suicide after the loss of his brother in a boating accident. She is like the other members of the Jarrett family—her husband Calvin and remaining son Conrad—in wanting to bypass such tragedies to become "ordinary" once again. In this story, "ordinary" equals perfect. It expresses a distinctive North American fantasy of perfection as the ordinary way of being, a peculiar notion that has become widely held in the last 150 years.[4] Writer Richard Fenn provides a sociological and theological analysis of this perfectionist impulse in British and American culture, "the dream of the perfect act" that fuses politics and the divine will.[5] John Shelton Lawrence and I dealt with the pop-culture side of this dream in *The American Monomyth*, an analysis of the superheroic figures whose perfect appearance and performance have dominated popular entertainment and advertisements since the 1930s.[6]

The theme of perfection, of course, has long held an important place in Christian theology. Methodist theologian Albert Outler argued that the Wesleyan doctrine of perfection was misunderstood early on as perfect performance and that Wesley's original conception was based on the Pauline conception of *teleios*, whose dynamic movement toward fulfillment was captured by the Eastern Fathers, on whom the early Wesleyan Holy Club at Oxford was modeled: "In this view, 'perfection' may be 'realized' in a given moment . . . , yet never in a finished state."[7] Later, this doctrine was interpreted as the possibility of perfection in the sense of "purity of intention" rather than perfection in performance. It is interesting to observe that the understanding of perfection in Pauline theology has been moving in the same relational and progressive direction.

What cultural analysts have discovered in recent decades, however, is that secularized forms of perfection are being felt more and more strongly in the consumer society. The American images of male and female perfection may be clarified by reflecting on the connections between Pauline theology and a story like *Ordinary People*.

The Metaphor of Flawed Vessels

Paul's idea of treasure in ordinary earthenware vessels was developed in response to the superapostles who had invaded Corinth and convinced the congregation that he was too flawed to be a true apostle. Compared with the perfect record that the superapostles claimed, Paul's record was that of a loser. Everything about his career and personal life seemed to belie the treasure of the gospel that he preached; if Jesus was indeed Lord, as he proclaimed, how could his servant be so weak and unimpressive?

To meet this challenge Paul created the metaphor of "earthen vessels."[8] Earthenware pots were as ubiquitous in a manufacturing and shipping center like Corinth as cardboard boxes in Chicago. Not only is the fragility of earthenware implied here but the cheapness[9] and disposability[10] of such containers. Compared with wooden boxes, which were expensive in antiquity, clay storage pots were literally dirt cheap. They were manufactured to rough specifications by the thousands. They were never perfectly round or precisely the same size. Lacking a glossy surface, they absorbed the odors or stains of stored products; one had to be careful that such odors and stains did not pollute future products stored in the same jar.[11] When they cracked, they could be clamped and used to store dry goods. When they shattered, they were thrown into the dump. As Barrett suggests in his commentary on this verse, Paul refers to the earthen vessels in the plural while the treasure remains in the singular, indicating that neither Paul nor his superapostle adversaries were invaluable nor perfect.[12] In fact, as John T. Fitzgerald's study of Corinthians has shown, Paul's metaphor implies that he is "quintessentially fragile."[13] The theological point of this metaphor is made clear in the second half of the verse: "to show the transcendent power belongs to God and not to ourselves."

This resonates with the basic theme of *Ordinary People*, the contrast between a flawed and vulnerable family and their attempt to be perfect. Like Paul being compared with the superapostles, the Jarretts are constantly comparing themselves and being compared with other families. Reluctantly they accept a dinner invitation from the Murrays, who live in an architectural prize-winning subdivision. Beth leaves the party in fury because Calvin revealed that their less-than-perfect son was still seeing a psychiatrist. She complains that it was a "violation of privacy . . . our privacy, the family's privacy." Compared with the super Murrays, they are flawed pots.[14] In the hyper-competitive atmosphere of an elite American suburb, this is utterly demoralizing.

Beth as "Harassed"

Paul's depiction of himself as "hard pressed" and "harassed" (2 Cor. 4:8–9) seems to describe Beth's experience of trying to live up to the expectations of feminine perfection. For a long time she had embodied what Jungian analyst Marion Woodman calls an "addiction to perfection."[15] Beth was admired by her peers as trim, athletic, well organized, and energetic. As the novel describes it, she spends long hours at the club organizing its national tennis tournament. Her fellow club members think of her as a miracle of efficiency. But inside she is different. Under the pressure of maintaining appearances after the death of a perfect son and the attempted suicide of his younger brother, she begins to crack. Holding herself rigidly against any emotion, the perfectionist breaks down into tears at unexpected moments. The film depicts her as a "wasp witch, whose face is so tense you expect it to break," to use film critic Pauline Kael's vivid words.[16] But the novel makes plain that behind her irritation toward husband and son is the attempt to maintain control, to preserve perfect ordinariness against threats on every side.

What made the appearance of orderliness so difficult to maintain, above all, was the way Conrad's attempted suicide was carried out. He had cut himself repeatedly, spreading blood all over Beth's immaculate bathroom carpet and tile. She perceived this as an assault on her perfect housekeeping; she also felt that her husband blamed her for the suicide, "for the whole thing." The expressions in our text that are translated as "hard pressed"[17] and "harassed" or persecuted[18] fit Beth's feelings very well, because she thinks of herself as unjustly blamed by her husband while being unfairly assaulted by her son. The outrageousness of her situation blocks the possibility of being comforted. Despite her efficient behavior and good intentions, the facade of perfect control has been undermined and she wants no encouragement to accept this situation as normal. As Calvin tells Beth in the film, the accident and attempted suicide "would have been all right if there hadn't been any mess. But you can't handle mess. You need everything neat and easy."

Vacation plans, a repeated source of conflict between Beth and Calvin, were for Beth a vehicle to escape the affliction and harassment of family life. She brings home travel brochures describing romantic escapes: "Christmas in London would be like something out of Dickens." Calvin resists being unavailable to their son during such a crucial period, especially since his suicide attempt had occurred after their last Christmas vacation trip. After they argue over their family obligations, the novel depicts Beth returning to the appeal of travel. She remembers the idyllic places they had visited and speaks of how good it feels "to get away." Behind this conversation lies a desperate yearning to escape troubles, to find ordinariness once again. Clay pots without glaze absorb gunk. But nothing sticks to the glossy photos of vacation brochures. Well-heeled tourists gaze on picturesque scenery and receive elegant service without being touched by the convoluted human stories all around them. They are far from the persons and places that remind them of their troubles at home. Touristic fun is the ultimate escape from the mess of ordinary entanglements.

It is fascinating to reflect on how the image of travel has changed from Paul's time to our own. Some of Paul's most prominent sources of "affliction" and "harassment" arose on journeys in an era before travel became safe and routine for tourists. In contrast to the allegedly trouble-free lives of the superapostles, Paul's life is revealed when he sums up his missionary career: "Three times I have been shipwrecked; a night and a day I have been adrift at sea; on frequent journeys, in danger from rivers, danger from robbers . . . danger in the city, danger in the wilderness, danger at sea . . . in toil and hardship, through many a sleepless night, in hunger and thirst, often without food, in cold and exposure" (2 Cor. 11:25–27). For Paul and most others in the Roman Empire, travel involved increased vulnerability. But for Beth, a wealthy North American, a vacation trip promises the absence of affliction and harassment, a temporary but blessed recovery of the glazed surface of ordinariness as perfection. But the larger truth about someone like Beth is stated by Marion Woodman: "Addiction to perfection is at root a suicidal addiction. . . . To move toward perfection is to move out of life, or what is worse, never to enter it."[19]

Calvin as "Perplexed"

Calvin Jarrett was also hung up on the expectation of polished performance, on matching a contemporary standard of masculine perfection, such as that described by Warren Farrell: "Perhaps the most prevailing expectation of men is our Superman expectation: the fear we are merely Clark Kents who won't be accepted unless we are a Superman. . . . Most men spend their lives performing—in sports, at sex, on the job—'proving ourselves' in one form or another."[20] To use Paul's terminology once again, Cal is "thrown into perplexity"[21] by the gaps between his standards and his performance. This dilemma is inadequately presented in the film, it seems to me. As a film critic observed, "Calvin isn't a character—he's just a blob created to be tyrannized by Beth."[22] But the novel offers access to his inner life. Confronting the responsibilities of fatherhood when his son returns from the mental institution, Calvin reflects that they seem "enormous. Staggering . . . this is the age of perfection. . . . Strive, strive. Correct all defects."[23]

Since the requirements of perfection seem impossible to fulfill, Calvin is left with perplexity on every hand. He notices a deterioration in his masculine self-image of always being on top of things at the office, at home, and in his athletic competitions. He blows a golf tournament that he could have won and is puzzled that somehow he did not expect to win. Calvin is perplexed over Beth's obsession with going on vacation trips, fearing a repetition of the previous year's suicide episode if they are not at home with their son at Christmas. He is torn about whether to feel responsible for the attempted suicide or not. He drinks too much in an effort to avoid what "he does not want to see."[24] He is aghast at wanting to strike out at his wife, "to knock the stubbornness out of her; him! The Clark Kent of Samuel Mumford High School, the model of gentleness as he had courted her."[25] Over and over again, he thinks his problems through "only to have the circuits blocked; the answers inaccessible."[26] Guest's novel allows us to overhear Calvin's realization that he had once been a perfectionist like his wife, but . . . "No more. Not since the summer before last and an unexpected July storm on Lake Michigan. He had left off being a perfectionist then, when he discovered that not . . . *anything* . . . cleared you through the terrifying office of chance; that it is chance and not perfection that rules the world."[27] If "your whole life is an accident," as Calvin says in the film, then what becomes of the certitudes that had been drummed into his consciousness at the evangelical orphanage and in the law school that had prepared him for success? He becomes distracted at work and preoccupied at home, leading Beth to query his friends about his being "out of focus" and "obsessed."[28]

Actually, Paul's term "perplexed" is more apt than the psychologically loaded term, "obsessed." The simplistic verities of ordinary life were shaken by tragedies. The script of ordinariness no longer functioned. The superapostles had promoted such a script in Corinth, claiming that true apostles of the transcendent Lord should be able to overcome any obstacles and avoid tragedy. When measured against this standard of superheroic perfection, Paul's career was perplexing indeed. Yet only by accepting perplexity could Paul discover the deeper meaning of faith.

Conrad as "Knocked Down"

Paul's final antithesis concerning the situation of "earthen vessels" describes the situation of Conrad as the imperfect son grappling with the death of an all-too-perfect brother. The J. B. Phillips translation of 2 Corinthians 4:9b translates Paul's clever wordplay into the language of prize fighting: "knocked down but not knocked out,"[29] which describes Conrad quite precisely. He describes his experience after the death of his brother as being like "falling into a hole and it keeps getting bigger and bigger . . . and you're trapped, and it's all over." He could not regain his equilibrium after the drowning of his elder brother. Although his brother was stronger and a better swimmer, he had finally let go of the overturned sailboat and drifted off into the storm, leaving Conrad with an intolerable burden of guilt and anger. The elder Jarrett son had been a popular athlete, the idol of the family, his mother's favorite. After the accident, Conrad was incapable of working through his grief at the loss of a seemingly flawless brother, and his relationships with his peers and his parents deteriorated and his schoolwork suffered. The straight-A student and champion swimmer drifted on a course toward failure and alienation, ending with the attempted suicide and a stay in a mental institution. The story fits the findings of an investigation that attempted to explain why adolescent suicides have increased 300 percent in the past quarter century, bringing rates in

North America to the top of the world scale. Suicide rates among college students, it found, frequently relate to the failure to live up to high academic expectations.[30] Pressures to succeed and to excel are related, in my opinion, to the pervasive perfectionism that marks the culture.

In the course of the story, Conrad gradually comes to terms with the pain of his past and present experiences. Until he is able to accept the fact that he was knocked off his feet for no particular fault of his own, he will remain unable to rise again. He feels that his mother hates him for surviving when his brother drowned. He expresses his anger at that by means of a suicidal gesture, and then blames her for being unloving thereafter. He is knocked down by grief and blame. The novel describes his feelings:

> The hammer blows of guilt and remorse. He has no weapons with which to fight them off. . . . He has pushed everyone away who tries to help. If he could apologize. . . . All connections with him result in failure. Loss. Evil.
>
> At school it is the same. Everywhere he looks, there is competence and good health. Only he, Conrad Jarrett, outcast, quitter . . . separated from everyone by this aching void of loneliness; but no matter, he deserves it.[31]

At the root of this separation and blame-setting is the conviction that disaster is not ordinary, that its pain must be assuaged by avoidance.

What Conrad discovers is that before you can get back on your feet again, it is necessary to admit the pain of being knocked down. Before earthen vessels can be useful in the wear and tear of daily life, their fragility must be recognized and respected. To admit the limitations of his family is to move beyond the setting of blame—of himself, his parents, or even of the strong elder brother who betrayed the moral universe by giving up in a storm.

The Psychiatrist in the Pauline Role

The figure who takes up Paul's line in *Ordinary People* is the psychiatrist, Dr. Tyrone Berger. No doubt the links I am describing to a religious model were not intended by Judith Guest, whose story is thoroughly secular.[32] Yet Berger's analysis of the problem shares the critique of perfectionism developed by the pastoral theologian William Stephens Taylor[33] and implied in Pauline theology. To use Pauline language, Berger advocates accepting the fragility of earthen vessels and rejects the hope of living successfully by conforming to the law. He takes the same attitude toward superheroic mastery as Paul does in the conflict with the invading apostles in Corinth.

When Conrad first visits Berger's office, he is struck with the doctor's rumpled appearance and the confusion in the room, which had been ransacked by an angry patient. When Conrad relates that he'd like to "be more in control. . . . So people can quit worrying about me," Berger places his cards on the table: "Well, I'll tell you something," Berger says. "I'm not big on control. But it's your money."

The problem with trying to control the breakability of earthen vessels is that it renders them dysfunctional. Berger contends that when pain and grief are suppressed, other life energies are diminished as well. He suggests there is a connection between control and lack of feeling. "Feelings are scary. Sometimes they're painful. And if you can't feel pain, then you're not going to feel anything else, either." This orientation leads to a simple but profound analysis of depression as "plain and simple *reduction of feeling*. . . . People who keep stiff upper lips find that it's damn hard to smile."[34] Berger's affirmation of bodily existence leads him to a thoroughly Pauline sense that the body is the true center of personhood and thus the surest indication of psychic health. "The body doesn't lie," Berger says. "You remember that. So all you gotta do is keep in touch."[35]

Although thoroughly secular in his language, Berger also shares Paul's critique of the law as a technique to guarantee that relationships will be successful. Conrad is discussing his reluctance to invite a girl out for a date. Guest's bumbling psychiatrist grins and says,

> "It's just like skiing. The first few times, you close your eyes and fake it, hope for the best."
> [Conrad replies,] "What do you know about skiing? Right from go, there are a million rules."
> Berger sighs. "Rules, again. They oughta burn every rule book that's ever been written!"
> "And where would we be?"
> "Out of the box!" He shakes his fists at the ceiling, in a parody of rage.[36]

To remain in the box is to remain alone, to invite death. "The written code kills," Paul wrote (2 Cor. 3:6). The "curse of the law" (Gal. 3:13) is that it separates performers from nonperformers, the acceptable from the nonacceptable. It locks people into the isolating chambers of blame. As long as the Jarretts remain confined by the law of suburban perfectionism, trying vainly to maintain a veneer of invulnerability, they are doomed. Their true selves and their unique relationships will have no chance to mature under pressure.

Berger's capacity to encourage the emergence of true personhood, with all its warts and vulnerabilities, is reminiscent of what Paul would call "love," the unmerited acceptance of others despite their flaws. Toward the end of the therapy process, Berger is grappling with Conrad's blaming of himself for his brother's drowning. The film has the boy exclaim, "It's got to be somebody's fault. . . . Why do things have to happen to people. It isn't fair." Berger agrees that it isn't fair, but to insist on a system of blame, in which life is measured out according to some socially acceptable standard of justice, is to close oneself off from the simple acceptance of oneself as an earthen vessel. To state the matter in Pauline terms, Conrad cannot find salvation through the law; he can find it only through grace. While the source of such grace is ambiguous in Guest's story, for Paul it arises from the cross and resurrection of Christ. That is what set him free from the bondage to blame, letting him know that despite his flaws and mistakes, he was unconditionally loved by God.

Hope for Ordinary People

Finally, let me touch on the positive outcome of the Jarretts' story. Despite their breakability, there is promise for those who recognize themselves as earthen vessels. In the end, Conrad discovers that although "knocked down," he is "not knocked out." To use the more literal translation of the Greek phrase used here, he is "not destroyed."[37] He discovers that suicide is not a necessary or appealing prospect. He begins to accept himself, including the worst of his feelings of grief, rage, and remorse. This involves acknowledging his own strength, because the source of his remorse was that he had hung on to the boat in the storm. Was this really so wrong? He begins to regain interest in his schoolwork and to feel more optimistic about his future. He gains a more balanced view of his parents and enters into a solid relationship with a girl in the school choir. When she becomes distraught over the arrival of the salesman from Ohio who had disrupted her parents' marriage, the novel makes it clear that Conrad can stand on his feet again. She looks to him for support and he is able simply to be there for her, which proves to be enough. His experience has rendered him capable of empathy because he knows that one can rise again after being crushed to the ground. "It's all right," he says. "It'll work out all right."[38]

Calvin finds that although "perplexed," he is not necessarily "driven to despair." He ends up resisting the conclusion that life is a series of accidents. He accepts Beth's need for space and time to work out her own accommodation with pain, acknowledging his own limitations as he thinks, *"you are not God, you do not know and you are not in control, so let go.*"[39] After falling down in the park while jogging, he decides to go talk with Dr. Berger. He admits that he had been wrong that "intelligent people can work out their problems." When Beth leaves home at the end of the story, Calvin is able to acknowledge that he doesn't fully understand why. He has overcome the fantasy of perfection as the ordinary way of being. And he is also certain that the simplistic mechanisms of blame are useless. "It's nobody's fault," he tells Conrad. "Things happen in this world. People don't always have the answers for them, you know." It is the same "lesson" that he has had to learn about the drowning and the attempted suicide. But this does not diminish his sense of responsibility and affection for his son, as conveyed in the powerful scene at the end of the film.

> "I'm not disappointed," Conrad says. "I love you."
> Calvin's eyes fill with tears as he hugs his son.
> "I love you, too."

One has the sense, at the end, of a father who has come to terms with his limitations and responsibilities, now ready, in Guest's words, "for whatever comes next."[40]

The novel also gives promise that while Beth has been "hard pressed" and "harassed," she need not feel "abandoned." While the cinematic version of *Ordinary People* gives no hope that Beth's travels away from her family will have positive results,[41] the novel ends with Conrad reflecting about the future. When his mother returns she will know "just as he does that it is love, imperfect and unordered, that keeps them apart, even as it holds them somehow together."[42] On the night before she left, Conrad comes downstairs to say he is happy to have his parents back from their trip. Conrad puts his arm around his mother in an awkward embrace to say goodnight. She looks off in the distance and then turns her head away as if to signal that his gesture had touched her very deeply. While it may take a while yet for her to understand and appreciate such affection, it is clear that she will not be forsaken by those who love her so imperfectly. The novel leaves us with the hope that Beth will ultimately understand that vulnerability is the mode for ordinary people. While the film offers no hope of Beth's transformation, it compensates with a hauntingly transcendent motif that is entirely lacking in the novel. The Pachelbel Canon in D sung by the high school choir recurs throughout the film, being heard the last time after Calvin's response to his son, "I love you, too." It offers a comforting hope for resolutions that may ultimately include everyone in the story.

So also Paul was preserved in his commitment to an honest, claylike acceptance of his own limitations within the context of divine love. As Fitzgerald shows, Paul's "human weakness is thus a foil for the glorification of God."[43] He persevered in his critique of the Corinthian superapostles who bragged about their possession of transcendent power. In the end the congregation woke up to the exploitative and illusionary implications of so culturally conditioned a system of conformity. They probably also came closer to grasping the paradox of faith in the shadow of the cross. We can at least hope that they ultimately understood Paul's words, "We always bear in our body the dying of Jesus, so that the life of Jesus may be displayed in our body" (2 Cor. 4:10).[44] Faith must always be embodied—in earthen vessels. Bodily vulnerability has been rendered acceptable by Christ's bodily death for the sake of others. The desperate drive to create the facade of perfection is no longer required. The "dying of Jesus" on the cross was an ultimate form of participation in bodily existence. On the cross the full measure of love for imperfect people was poured out. So as Christians accept themselves as earthen vessels hallowed by the treasure of unmerited love, they may experience the true "life of Jesus" in the thick confusion of bodily existence. Believers thereby demonstrate the divinely ordained freedom from the tyranny of blame and perfectionism that have the tendency to transform persecution, perplexity, harassment, and hard knocks into distorting, dehumanizing burdens.

Finally, I think there is reason to believe that Paul's calm acceptance of bodily vulnerability allowed him to face the extremity of his own life with a measure of equanimity. Years earlier he had faced death in the hope that "with full courage now as always Christ will be honored in my body, whether by life or by death. For to me to live is Christ, and to die is gain" (Phil. 1:20–21). When the end finally came, it was on a deserted road outside the walls of Rome where summary executions were conducted without trial or ceremony.[45] He must have known as he knelt for the executioner's sword that no believer would be present to place earthenware shards over his eyes after death or to toss the ritual handful of dirt into the grave, fulfilling the ancient customs. There would be no ceremonies. His body would be tossed into an unconsecrated grave at the roadside. But Paul no longer required additional hands to convey acceptance of the divinely appointed order of earthen vessels: "ashes to ashes, dust to dust." Ever since the crisis with the superapostles, he had been reconciled to living as a flawed vessel. The earthenware apostle crumbled alongside a distant Roman road but the treasure still remains.

9

Empire of the Sun and the Death of Innocence

For by the grace given to me I enjoin every one who is
among you,
> do not be superminded beyond what one ought to
> be minded,
but set your mind on being soberminded,
> according to the measuring rod of faith that God dealt out
> to each.

(Rom. 12:3)

In this effort to relate Paul to American culture, I have frequently touched on the theme of superheroism. In the
light of a well-known but little-understood text from Romans, I would like to analyze the Superman fantasy and its
demise in the film *Empire of the Sun*.[1] The potential of this
text has long been obscured by the smoothing-out of the
translation process. It is usually translated, "I bid every one
among you not to think of himself more highly than he
ought to think, but to think with sober judgment, each according to the measure of faith which God has assigned
him" (RSV). No one would imagine from this version that
the verse contains an elaborate play on the word "be
minded," with the Greek element *phronein* appearing four

times with various prefixes. With the literal translation printed above, a surprising and significant antithesis between supermindedness and sobermindedness becomes clear. Here Paul is tapping a tradition of Greek philosophy and literature that reaches back to the beginnings of the Western heritage. This Jewish thinker, who expressed himself caustically on more than one occasion about the vanity of contemporary philosophy, uses in this crucial location a term that Helen North has extensively analyzed in her book *Sophrosyne: Self Restraint in Greek Literature*. The contrast between sobermindedness and what we might call the superheroic principle, she argues, "lies at the very heart of Hellenism."[2] Her study allows us to connect Paul's use of these terms with an age-old struggle between superheroism and mortality, between the effort to transcend all human limitations, and the sober acknowledgment of limits.

To connect what Paul was writing to the Romans with American culture, I would like to relate it to two pieces of modern imagination. An issue of *Time* in 1988 carried one of these artifacts on its cover. Superman is taking off the Clark Kent suit under a headline, "He's 50!" The thought caption to the left of the familiar, muscular figure contains the challenge that touches every one of us sooner or later: "Strange . . . I've vanquished every crook, spy and weirdo with my supernatural powers, but dealing with the big five-oh may be my biggest challenge yet . . . ! ! !"[3] As the feature story points out, since the Superman character was created fifty years ago and appeared in the first issue as a young man of twenty-five, "he would actually now be 75, his superbody weak and weary, his X-ray vision dimmed. But since he still looks about 25, he can be said to be timeless, immortal."[4] The fictional Superman doesn't really have to worry about the ravages of time as others do. Like the early Christians whom Paul addressed, Americans yearn for that status of timeless innocence. The *Time* article describes it:

> Superman . . . manages to embody the best qualities
> in that nebulous thing known as the American charac-

ter. He is honest . . . he is idealistic and optimistic, he helps people in need. He not only fights criminals but is indifferent to those vices that so often lead the rest of us astray. . . . He is not vain. He is not greedy. . . . He does not lust after power. And not only is he good, he is also innocent in a kind and guileless way that Americans have sometimes been but more often have only imagined themselves to be.[5]

Here we find the contrast that Paul was dealing with, the tendency to consider oneself and one's group to be super. The vision of innocence is beguiling.

The healthy side of Paul's contrast is wonderfully embodied in another piece of popular entertainment. Steven Spielberg's film *Empire of the Sun*, based on a screenplay developed by Tom Stoppard, offers a resource to deal with a necessary and healthy death of innocence. Although some film critics panned it for going too much against the stream, Vincent Canby named it "the best film ever made about childhood by a director born and bred in this country."[6] It is a distinctively American treatment of a universal issue.

The story of *Empire of the Sun* is based on the novel by that title written by J. G. Ballard, who experienced the Shanghai of 1941 as a British schoolboy. The twelve-year-old Jim is pictured as a privileged member of a private school in Shanghai. He undergoes the upheaval of the Japanese invasion and grows through young adolescence in a Japanese internment camp, separated from his parents. His boyhood fantasy centers on superheroic flight: he loves airplanes and heroic pilots, whether they were Japanese or American. Even the question of the existence of God is related to planes, as Jim queries his mother early in the film, "Is God above us; does it mean up, like flying?"[7] The underlying theme of the movie is very close to Paul's admonition in Romans 12:3, though Ballard, Spielberg, and Stoppard are unlikely to have been conscious of the parallels.

The innocence of superheroic flight stands in tension with the requirements of mature moderation or "soberminded-ness." According to the film, this type of maturity is possible only when one abandons the alluring dream of superheroism.

The Ancient Peril of Supermindedness

To understand what is at stake here, I need to take you on a brief trip through the history of ideas that lies behind Paul's contrast between supermindedness and soberminded-ness. In the archaic and heroic periods of Greek culture, Helen North argues, there was a contrast between two types of heroes.[8] The "megalo-psycho" hero, the "high minded" or superhero, was exemplified by Ajax or Achilles, figures whose passion for honor led them to violate customs. In contrast, the moderate hero like Odysseus accepted limits, shrewdly acted to preserve the lives of his colleagues within such limits, and prevailed by avoiding *hubris*, pride. The significance of the distinction between supermindedness and sobermindedness was enhanced by connections with the Greek religious tradition. Both the worship of Apollo and the Delphic oracles stressed the central principle "Know thyself . . . that thou art but mortal." Within this context, sobermindedness came to be seen as the virtue of the person who knows he or she is not a god or goddess.

The social setting of this emphasis was the Greek city-state of the seventh through the fifth centuries B.C., in which the unlimited drive for power and success was perceived to be the greatest danger. A similar warning by the poet Alcman of that period, "Let no man soar to the heavens nor try to wed Aphrodite, the Queen of Paphos," had a political significance.[9] It resisted the pretensions of super-heroic individuals whose deeds could endanger the city, since as North suggests, "only by taming the hero could the community grow."[10] The first half of the Alcman saying expresses the warning not to try flying like Superman, so to speak. Don't seek to be above others, don't rise too far beyond traditional customs. The second half of the saying resists the opposite but profoundly related tendency of viewing oneself as a victim whose life problems can be solved by marrying a god or goddess, or by inviting such a person to be one's political leader. It was out of this complex of ideas that the Greeks came to consider pride as "the characteristic vice of tyrants" and its opposite, *sophrosyne* or sobermindedness, as "the virtue of the constitutional form of government which overthrows or wards off tyranny."[11]

The curious thing is that this powerful distinction passed out of common usage long before Paul's time. The soberminded person came to be viewed as the one turned toward the divine, partaking of the divine nature and so forth. It is therefore curious that Paul's usage in Romans 12—and 2 Corinthians 5:13—stood closer to early Greek thought than to the usage of his own time. In part the reason was that the problems Paul faced in the early church were similar to those that arose in the early Greek democracies. Charismatic religious experiences led members to overweening pride that was fed by powerful first-century trends like Gnosticism and popular political myths. The superheroic images of figures larger than life, born of the fusion of human and divine beings, were as important to the popular imagination of the first century as they had been in the heroic period centuries earlier. The message of the culture was similar to that of our own: either be an innocent superstar or an innocent victim rescued by a superstar.

When Paul states that every Christian should seek sobermindedness rather than supermindedness, he was warding off the popular philosophy and the mythological heritage of his era that tended to slip through the cracks of the redeemed community. He was pointing to the danger of individuals modeling themselves after the gods of popular mythology or the political leaders celebrated in the civic cults and public festivals in Rome. He had learned from bitter experience in the tumultuous churches of Thessalonica and Corinth that persons who think they are gods and goddesses become impossible to live with, that the Christian community can be preserved only at the price of taming the superheroes. He discovered that those claiming superheroic innocence cause havoc in human relationships: they blunder about, ruining institutions, but seem incapable of recognizing what they have done. They blithely move on through the wreckage they have caused, believing that the failure of cooperation is always someone else's fault while they themselves are as much the embodiment of innocence as Superman.

This helps us relate a film like *Empire of the Sun* to Paul's message in Romans. The film represents Steven Spielberg's effort to move past the superheroic fantasies of his earlier, and more widely popular, films. In an interview, Spielberg described the odyssey that led him from superheroic tales like *Close Encounters of the Third Kind, Raiders of the Lost Ark, E. T., Back to the Future, Gremlins,* and *Goonies* to this more realistic kind of film. *Empire of the Sun* represents Spielberg's maturing attraction "to the idea that this was a death of innocence."[12] The film shows Jim gradually facing the reality of evil, not only in the Japanese brutality and in the callousness it produced in the inmates but also in the great burst of light he saw in the summer of 1945, over distant Nagasaki. Spielberg said, "I wanted to draw a parallel story between the death of this boy's innocence and the death of the innocence of the entire world."[13]

Supermindedness rejects responsibility for evil. It preserves an image of innocence at the price of denying the truth of the universal human condition, that all families and companies and churches and nations are touched in various ways with complicity. In contrast with the superheroic myths of ancient and modern fantasies, not every form of ill fortune is imposed by malicious outsiders. The healthy alternative is to be "soberminded," with a realistic sense of limitations and involvement in ambiguity and evil. For as Romans 3:23 had shown, all humans without exception "have sinned and fall short of the glory of God." If Paul is right, innocence is an illusion that needs to die.

The Shape of Sobermindedness

If supermindedness is to be abandoned, then what is the shape of the sobermindedness that Paul recommends? It is very different from the cynical outlook of those who have simply abandoned superheroic expectations because they have been disappointed or disillusioned. It is grounded in faith in the crucified and risen Christ. Paul states the healthy alternative this way: "but set your mind on being soberminded, each according to the measuring rod of faith that God has assigned." The idea here is that each member of the Christian community is given a measuring rod, a standard of faith that comes from personal and corporate experience to guide our understanding of Christ.[14] There is a bracing element of personal autonomy in this concept: every person in the church has such a measuring rod, according to Paul. If differing theological measuring rods have equal validity, and if no group can legitimately impose its standards on others, this means that people no longer have to view themselves as victims or vanquishers, winners or losers.

The letter to the Romans was directed to house churches whose measuring rods were sufficiently different that they were engaged in battles for primacy. Conservatives were vying with liberals, Jewish Christians against Gentile Christians, each attempting to make their measuring rod into a super standard that should be accepted by all. It is a battle that has continued in Christianity ever since, because groups have usually forgotten to link their theological measuring sticks with the command of sobermindedness. Denominational traditions, including my own Wesleyan heritage with all its richness and promise, are limited in scope. They are not suited for everyone, and there are other measuring rods of faith with equal claims to validity. For the sake of honesty and to preserve the humanity of Christian groups in Rome, Paul urges that they cease acting as if their measuring rod alone were legitimate. All people of faith "see through a glass darkly," as Paul insists in 1 Corinthians 13. Theological and moral insights are always partial, no matter how inspired in origin or eloquent in presentation.

A major problem with supermindedness is that such limitations are overlooked. We see this clearly in the Superman myth that has been so pervasively a part of the education of contemporary Americans. Not only is Superman presented as "timeless" and "immortal," to use the terms of *Time* magazine. The *Time* writer observes that "In his extraterrestrial origins and the shining purity of his altruism, some commentators have detected a divine aura."[15] He is a kind of angel figure, capable of flight and ethereal purity. It is also striking to observe how the story line of Superman corresponds to that of Christ. "Screenwriter Newman sees yet more exalted implications in the [Superman] legend. 'It begins with a father who lives up in heaven, who says, "I will send my only son to save earth." The son takes on the guise of a man but is not a man. The religious overtones are so clear.'"[16]

Christopher Reeve, who played the Superman role in the recent films, goes so far as to speak of the real-life redemptive power of this fantasy. "It's very hard for me to be silly about Superman," he said, "because I've seen firsthand how he actually transforms people's lives. I have seen children dying of brain tumors who wanted as their last request to talk to me, and have gone to their graves with a peace brought on by knowing that their belief in this kind of character is intact. I've seen that Superman really matters."[17] Here is a form of faith that perceives the transcendent power to be readily available in a fantasy figure. Sobermindedness is abandoned. Here is a redeemer who will surely cure America of victimage, even if everyone can't become super beings themselves.

Abandoning Two Forms of Innocence

This is why I find *Empire of the Sun* so powerful an alternative to the Superman mentality. Rather than allowing the superheroic pilots and rescuers to retain the immortal aura they possess in all of his earlier films, here Spielberg shows their limitation by juxtaposing them against a truly transcendent frame. The film begins with a haunting arrangement of the Welsh hymn "Suo Gan," sung by a boys choir, and ends with an equally stirring "Adoramus Te." Neither of these components that frame the film are in Ballard's novel. This is the first of several instances of what John Lawrence and I called "Mythic Alchemy,"[18] the process by which the transition from print to the cinematic medium is guided by the embodiment of a predominant mythic paradigm. In this film, the alchemy transforms a potentially superheroic story into its sober opposite. The music inserts an element of genuinely transcendent faith as a backdrop for Jim's gradual abandonment of superheroic fantasies. I believe this provides a clue to the maturation that comes through his experiences in the internment camp.

The film depicts Jim's gradual disillusionment with two forms of innocence: superheroism and super villainy. The first form is the superheroism of the Japanese and American pilots. Both the novel and the film depict Jim's fascination with the pure discipline and daring of the fighter pilots. Jim wishes that he had been among the Japanese pilots who destroyed the Allied ships at Pearl Harbor and in the China Sea.[19] He is particularly attracted to the kamakazi pilots, whose heroism and youth are so starkly visible. But he also cheers the Allied pilots who sweep over the airbase later in the film in their P-38s and P-51s. An element of mythic alchemy is present in the kamikaze rituals watched by Jim in the film, contrasting with Ballard's depiction of "the threadbare ceremonies that took place beside the runway."[20] The film has Jim add his haunting boy soprano voice to the Japanese ceremonies, assimilating them somehow into the transcendent frame with which the film begins and ends. His song is a haunting elegy that celebrates the passing of the purest form of Japanese innocence.

An opposite form of innocence is found in the exploitative prisoner Basie, played by John Malkovich. This American sailor manages to prosper in the internment camp by refined criminality, gathering a circle of henchmen who extort and steal from other prisoners. He is the ultimate rip-off artist, motivated purely by the desire for profit and the comforts it affords and teaching a doctrine of pure selfishness. Jim becomes Basie's errand boy, reveling in the sense of amoral freedom it affords.[21] He learns Basie's philosophy: "Buyin' and sellin'—life. Keep the ball in play; get first in line." It is the quintessential form of ruthless, American capitalism. Jim's subservience to Basie even including risking his life to inspect some pheasant traps placed in the forbidden zone just outside the camp, which turned out to be Basie's way of keeping track of a sure escape route when things become desperate in the internment camp.

A crucial moment in Spielberg's film comes when Jim and his fellow prisoners are led out of the camp by their Japanese captors in search of food supplies. Each person is allowed to take one suitcase along. Spielberg lets the audience see the mementos that Jim lovingly keeps in his kit, including a model of a Japanese Zero fighter, a "Wings" comic book of the superheroic type, a Norman Rockwell poster showing a mother hovering over her children, and a "Four Freedoms" poster promising rescue for the helpless. The contrast with Ballard's novel is striking at this point. Ballard depicts the treasured possessions in a traditional European context of imagination: "a Japanese cap badge given to him by Private Kimura; three steel-bossed fighting tops; a chess set and a copy of Kennedy's Latin primer . . . ; his Cathedral School blazer, a carefully folded memory of his young self; and the pair of clogs he had worn for the past three years.[22] Through the process of mythic alchemy, Spielberg transformed this suitcase into a symbol of superheroic fantasies.

So when Jim casts the bag into the river in the exhaustion of the trek away from the internment camp, it constitutes a turn from supermindedness to sobermindedness.

In subsequent events this symbolic antithesis is embodied in cinematic actions. Jim is led to see the failure of innocent superheroics, innocent victimage, and innocent exploitation. He and the starving Mrs. Victor remain behind the rest of the internees, pretending they are dead. She dies the next morning and Jim sees the great flash of light over distant Japan, only later to discover that it was not Mrs. Victor's soul going up to heaven. After his friend, the childlike kamikaze pilot, was shot by Basie and his marauding ex-prisoner friends, Jim tries frantically to pound the pilot's heart to bring him back to life as the doctor had demonstrated in the prison hospital. "I can bring everyone back, everyone; I can bring everyone back," Jim says over and over after gazing at the sunlight through his fingers and remembering the flash of the atomic bomb.[23] The mythic alchemy is particularly complex at this point, because the parallel episode in the novel is a macabre incident in which Jim slips a morsel of Spam into the mouth of a dead Japanese pilot only to find he is still alive. The shock and revulsion lead him to fantasize being able to raise the dead of the war, but he quickly abandons the thought and moves on to save himself.[24] The film shows more decisively than the novel that the era of superheroics is over, both for the boy-pilot and for the countless other victims of war's carnage. Unlike the episode in *Superman: The Movie,* where Superman made time go backward to resurrect Lois Lane, in this film Jim does not possess the superheroic strength to bring the dead back to life.

Jim also comes to discern the truly bestial shape of the Basie mentality: looking out for number one proves to be death-dealing and destructive of all that Jim loves. The passive role he had been playing for years with Basie proves futile and repulsive. When Basie pulls Jim away from the dead Japanese pilot he was trying to resuscitate and says, "Say, haven't you learned anything from me?" Jim replies with scorn, "Yes, that people will do anything for a potato." He refuses to stay with Basie and his gang, returning alone to the empty internment camp.

Jim also finds that the role of passive victim is equally and bafflingly empty. He tries to "surrender" to the American occupation troops just as he had to the Japanese years earlier. In neither case was he successful. In this film, life experiences resolutely run counter to the hope of co-opting victimage. So when Jim meets his parents again at the end of the film and prepares to board the ship for the England he scarcely remembers, it is clear that he is a completely different boy than he was when the film began. The road to growing up is seen to run past the shattering of illusions.

The Renunciation of Innocence

In the closing scene of the film, after Jim is reunited with the parents he hardly recognizes after so long a time, the camera pans the misty and turgid river to spy his wooden suitcase one last time, drifting into oblivion. This is a climactic instance of mythic alchemy, encouraging viewers to move beyond superheroic innocence. The closing scene of Ballard's novel is a nameless child's coffin floating on the river past Shanghai. Its paper flowers are shaken loose by the landing craft carrying Allied sailors back to their ships after they had insulted the Chinese by forming a chorus line outside the Shanghai Club and urinating down the front steps. This gives the Jim of the novel a sobering premonition of future retribution: "One day China would punish the rest of the world and take a frightening revenge."[25] But with Spielberg's unerring alchemy, this episode with Jim's box in the water becomes instead a symbol of the abandonment of the illusion of superheroic innocence. This completes the cinematic transformation of Ballard's novel into a profound moral and spiritual statement to America in the late decades of the twentieth century. Quite in line with Paul's contrast between superheroics and sobermindedness, the filmmaker challenges our culture to overcome the fantasies that have led us unknowingly into futile behavior, blocking our maturation.

During the last several decades, American culture has abandoned itself to dreams of innocence. We demand that our president be a superstar and we love to play the role of the innocent nation defending innocent victims. There is a need to load such illusions into a favorite suitcase now and toss them into the river. Americans cannot be soberminded while harboring superminded dreams of innocence, for themselves or for the groups to which they belong. The measuring rod of true faith in the crucified Christ can provide courage to face the truth, to reject the illusions of innocence that block the future. It is time to sing the Te Deum to the true God of the universe, gaining thereby the capacity to grow up and face responsibilities. The gates of the internment camp that aided our maturation are ajar now. Like Jim, we may be tempted to return to that strange, constricted realm where our daydreams spread their languid wings. But the war is over now. It is time to board the ship for the home we never really knew.

10

The Disguise of Vengeance
in *Pale Rider*

Beloved, do not avenge yourselves,
    but give way to the wrath [of God],
for it is written,
    "Vengeance is for me, I will repay,"
        says the Lord.
But if "your enemy is hungry, feed him;
    if he is thirsty, give him drink;
        for by doing this you will pile up burning coals
        upon his head."
Do not be conquered by the evil
    but conquer the evil with the good.[1]

(Rom. 12:19–21)

Paul's warning against vengeance was countered several years ago by a widely shared sentiment regarding the capture of a mass murderer in the city where I live. After a killing spree through the Midwest, Alton Coleman was captured without resistance by police in Evanston. A professional woman stated the view that many others held: "I wish he had been killed in a shootout with the police!" Vengeance—quick and final—is a yearning that has assumed a most peculiar form in our society, whose popular

118

myths lead us to prefer to have the police act as avenging judges and executioners. This popular preference for shoot-outs that result in the deaths of criminals is expressed in classical form in *Pale Rider*,[2] with Clint Eastwood playing the role of the nameless stranger who rids a small town of its murderous predators in the employ of a ruthless mining corporation. Since the stranger had earlier been gunned down by the same predators, there is an element of personal vengeance disguised by this traditional tale of selfless re-demption of a helpless community. The movie has some fascinating links with Romans 12–13 that may shed light on how to counter the siege of violence that threatens to en-gulf the country.

Vengeance and Vigilantism

"Beloved, do not avenge yourselves," writes Paul to the Roman Christians. It is an admonition that seems flatly to counter the sentiments expressed about an American serial killer. But rather than condemning those who feel the need for direct and effective vengeance in the case of particularly heinous criminals, I would like to explore the cultural origin of this sentiment. It can be traced back to early American traditions of using violent stories from the Bible to justify taking the law into one's own hands. Derived from biblical stories such as that of Phinehas the lyncher in Numbers 25, an ideal of holy vengeance has long existed in our society. Acting on the premise that God inspires and justifies the righteous to take vengeance in his behalf, we have cele-brated a succession of heroes who took the law into their own hands—from the disguised citizens of the Boston Tea Party through John Brown in his Harper's Ferry raid, from the Phantom and Dick Tracy through the Avengers of con-temporary comics.

The vigilante ethos justifies direct violence so long as the evil is clear-cut, the vigilantes are disinterested, and their identity is kept secret. The appeal of this vigilante tradition has been that quick vengeance could be achieved for crimes that might otherwise go unpunished. The belief is that this could be done by agents sufficiently disguised so as to prevent the risk of feuds or reprisals.

To understand how citizens could prefer that the defenders of the law sometimes take the law into their own hands and execute vengeance on criminals requires a grasp of the widely popular myth system that developed in the wake of the vigilante tradition. The many popular superheroes in modern entertainment derive from earlier forms of the cowboy and detective stories that have embodied this vigilante plot.

A crucial example of this kind of story is *The Virginian*, Owen Wister's 1902 novel, which contained the first Main Street duel in American literature.[3] The story is set in the context of the struggles in Wyoming between farmers and ranchers, specifically the range war in Johnson County in which lynching and systematic thievery practiced by both sides came to a climax in 1892. The ranchers imported a trainload of Texas gunmen equipped with dynamite to put down the resistance of the farmers who were homesteading land in the public domain that the ranchers had used without rent for years. Widespread violence came to a climax near Buffalo, Wyoming, where federal troops finally intervened.

Wister romanticized the ranchers' side of this struggle in the creation of the Virginian, a tall, nameless cowboy who became the foreman of Sunk Creek Ranch. He was forced to track down a rustling gang, capturing two of its members, one of whom was formerly his best friend. True to the vigilante code, the Virginian renounced friendship and had the thieves hung. The chief rustler, Trampas, escaped with a guileless sidekick. When the trackers approached, Trampas shot him in the back so he could escape on their only horse.

Several years later Trampas is seen by the Virginian and his fiancée, Molly, a schoolteacher. She comments that it seems "wicked that this murderer" should go free when others were hanged for rustling. "He was never even arrested," says the girl. "No, he helped elect the sheriff in that county," replies the Virginian.

In the dramatic climax of the novel, which became required reading for high school classes all over America, the rustler issues a formal challenge for a Main Street duel. The Virginian sought the counsel of the clergyman who was to perform the wedding ceremony. The bishop was convinced that the rustlers had to be dealt with by vigilante tactics, that "they elected their men to office, and controlled juries; that they were a staring menace to Wyoming. His heart was with the Virginian. But there was his Gospel that he preached, and believed, and tried to live." He reminds the Virginian of the biblical injunction not to kill. The heroic cowboy responds, "Mighty plain to me, seh. Make it plain to Trampas, and there'll be no killin.'" As they parry about the contradictory demands of religion and law, the Virginian poses the key question: "How about instruments of Providence, seh?" In other words, what about the biblical idea of providence taking the form of heroic vigilantes who rid the world of evildoers? As the hero reluctantly departs for the duel that threatens to end his hoped-for marriage and even his life, the bishop finds he cannot repress the words, "God bless him! God bless him!"

Everyone knows the end of the story, even without having read *The Virginian* or seen the film in which Gary Cooper played the title role. In the archetypal duel with Trampas, the bad guy draws and shoots first, but is killed by the Virginian's bullets. The hero's friends marvel, "You were that cool! That quick!" which expresses the cool ethos of the vigilante tradition. The state of Wyoming is redeemed from the threat of crime because vengeance has occurred. Molly's New England conscience that had resisted the vigilante tactic so strongly finally relents, and she marries the Virginian. The novel ends with the hero and his family ensconced in prosperity. The Virginian becomes a wealthy rancher and mine owner, passing the redemptive task on to the next generation.

This novel had hundreds of imitations, including *Pale Rider*. Shortly after the cinematic triumph of *The Virginian* in 1929, it was followed by the emergence of serialized stories featuring the supercowboy the Lone Ranger, the supercop Dick Tracy, and superheroes like Superman, Wonderwoman, and Captain America, in tales that embody the same kind of plot. It is one of the most pervasive tales in American culture,[4] giving shape to the yearning for quick and effective public vengeance outside legally limited public means. Here is vengeance without due process of law, yet done with dignity and heroic self-restraint. The public does not take the law into its own hands in this kind of story. "Instruments of providence" take up the task of the "wrath of God," which Paul believed should never be shouldered by people in their own behalf.

The result of this widely popular myth is that it allows Americans to imagine gaining vengeance without using their own private means. They gain in fantasy a perfect form of public vengeance but never feel the need to name it as such. It is disguised as a story of courageous redemption of helpless communities by selfless heroes. This kind of story has the immense advantage of proceeding without the slow and cumbersome machinery of public means in a constitutional society. The United States has police forces without judicial powers, a court system bound by constitutional restraints, and forms of punishment that often seem awkward and ineffective. Compared with this, who would not prefer the "miracle" of a *Pale Rider?*

Cinematic Miracles as Disguised Vengeance

Megan Wheeler is burying her puppy after the marauders hired by the mining corporation had made yet another raid on the defenseless miners at Carbon Canyon. She breaks off the recitation of the Twenty-third Psalm to look skyward: "But they killed my dog! Why did you let them kill my dog?" When there is no reply from the heavens, she returns to the psalm: "For thou art with me. Thy rod and thy staff comfort me—but we need more than comfort. We need a miracle. . . . Mother says miracles happen, sometimes. The book says they happen."[5] On her way back from the hillside grave, the girl sees a horseman with a broad-brimmed hat riding slowly into town. It is, of course, Clint Eastwood, playing the role of "the Preacher," who ultimately takes his .44 caliber pistol out of storage to redeem the community from its corporate outlaws.

On one level, the redemption promised by *Pale Rider* seems to fit the parameters of the divine "wrath" that Paul hopes will be provided in the place of human vengeance. When the stranger rescues one of the beleaguered miners from three of the hired gunmen, he is invited to Megan's home for supper. After cleaning up from his redemptive exertions, the stranger appears with a clerical collar. Everyone else is stunned that so skilled a fighter could be a preacher— everyone except Megan. "She knew a miracle when she met one."[6] Later she describes the uncanny stranger with a line from the book of Revelation that suggests the title of the movie: "And I looked, and beheld a pale horse: and his name that sat on him was death, and hell followed with him" (Rev. 6:8). The tall stranger demonstrates a miraculous ability to prevail against the bullies hired by the mining corporation, smashing them with effortless ease in encounter after encounter. His presence in Carbon Canyon causes an incredible revival of morale as the miners set about restoring their homes and mining sluices. He reappears with uncanny timing to rescue Megan from a gang rape at the hands of the corporate thugs and acts as a divinely appointed judge to dynamite the mining operation that destroys entire hillsides and valleys with its gigantic water cannon. This "god of some sort"[7] prevails against incredible odds in the final duel against a gang of hired gunmen, killing them all with the relentless accuracy of an apocalyptic avenger.

The profile of the gunmen hired to contend with the tall preacher matches the biblical archetype of agents of the antichrist. "The enemy is the devil himself. . . . Even the villainous lawman's name, Stockburn, conjures up flames," a reviewer wrote.[8] The six gunmen along with Stockburn are made to appear like some seven horsemen of the apocalypse. Alan Dean Foster's novelization of the film provides this chilling description of the scene in front of Stockburn's headquarters when the corporation's telegram arrives to summon the angels of destruction into battle:

> There were seven horses tied to the hitching rail that fronted the lawman's office. Each had a black saddle on its back. A black leather rifle holster slashed at an angle on the right-hand side of each seat. Their oiled walnut stocks gleaming, seven Winchesters filled the holsters. Expensive guns, worth a lot of money in a bustling frontier community like Yuba City. They sat there in plain sight, apparently unguarded. There was nothing to prevent a resourceful thief from making off with the lot of them.
>
> Nothing except knowing better.[9]

When they arrive in the mining community, the gunmen begin by shooting down an unarmed miner with uncanny coordination and accuracy. After making him dance in the streets for a while by firing at his feet, Stockburn gives a slight nod and all seven guns fire simultaneously into his defenseless body. It is the kind of law that the preacher had explained to the miners after they decided to refuse the offer to be bought out by the corporation. "I don't know how he ever managed to get himself appointed Marshal, but that doesn't matter. . . . Stockburn's got six deputies been with him a long time. Six—and they'll uphold whatever law pays them the most. Killing's their way of life."[10] The model for this kind of figure within the Pauline tradition is the "lawless one" who usurps the place of a properly lawful agent, deluding people "with all power and with pretended signs and wonders, and with all wicked deception"(2 Thess. 2:9). So it seems appropriate that these evil gunmen are slain in the end by divine agency, fulfilling the biblical paradigm (2 Thess. 2:8). In the most incredible duel scene in the history of Westerns, the preacher alone prevails in a Main Street face-off with all seven killers, who come within twenty-three yards before anyone fires. It was the final miracle, without any doubt, achieved by more than human powers. This is probably the reason the "Inspirational Films" lobby group touted the "positive Christian values" in *Pale Rider*.[11]

Yet there is a major discrepancy in this picture of impartial, superheroic redemption. After all of his partners are killed by the tall stranger, Stockburn is cut down by a hail of bullets, fired more quickly than even the most experienced gunman could get off a single shot. "The shells ripped an eight-inch circle into the Marshal's chest."[12] This odd detail matches the strange sight caught by the camera earlier in the movie while the preacher was washing up for dinner in the Wheelers' home. The scars on his back

> would have caught the eye of the most indifferent observer. There were five of them. Each was a half inch in diameter and evenly spaced from its neighbor. They formed a neat circle. Though long since healed over, their origin was unmistakeable.
> They were bullet holes.[13]

This explains why Stockburn suddenly recognized the tall stranger in the duel scene, having earlier dismissed reports of similarities to someone he used to know. "Couldn't be him," Stockburn had told his corporate employer earlier in the story, because the "man I'm thinking about is dead."[14] Stockburn had evidently fired that circle of bullets in the back of the tall stranger and left him for dead.[15] The duel on Main Street was therefore an act of personal vengeance. As the tall stranger explained before the battle, "It's an old score. There's more to it than the problems of the folks in Carbon Canyon. Time's come to settle things."[16] So the superhero tale disguises what really amounts to private vengeance, carried out in a precise fashion of tit for tat, an eye for an eye, and a tooth for a tooth. The symmetry is almost biblical, a kind of holy battle against a demonic enemy who receives a precisely measured retribution. Yet the greatness of this particular Clint Eastwood film is that the disguise is fleetingly lifted. Behind the superheroic story, with all its apocalyptic references to the pale horse of the book of Revelation, there lies a tale of personal vengeance.[17]

Moving Past Vengeance

The relation between Paul's view in Romans and the view popularized in the American entertainment system gains cogency because Paul was facing similar myths in the first century. In particular, large segments of the Jewish community in the period prior to the Jewish-Roman war of A.D. 66–70 favored a vigilante strategy. Modeling their behavior on the same heroic tales in the Old Testament that inspired early vigilantes in our society, zealous Jews believed that their violence against evildoers would achieve divine ends. In particular these advocates of Jewish vigilantism felt that the Roman governing authorities should be opposed on principle, and with force. And it was natural in this kind of environment that many persons who had suffered injustices at the hands of the authorities felt themselves called by the heroic myths to take the law into their own hands, to avenge themselves and thus to avenge Israel.

It is in this context that Paul's admonition "Beloved, never avenge yourselves, but leave it to the wrath of God" (Rom. 12:19, RSV) assumes significance. He was tapping the ancient tradition of never being a judge in one's own cause, a principle embodied in Jewish as well as Greco-Roman law. It is a crucial principle as well for modern jurisprudence.

The trouble with the police or private citizens taking the law in their own hands is that the omniscience and impartiality of the myths such as *The Virginian* and the *Pale Rider* rarely work out in reality. Zealotism is presumptuous, Paul implies here, for it refuses to "give way" to the prerogatives of divine justice: "leave it to the wrath of God; for it is written, 'Vengeance is mine, I will repay, says the Lord'" (Rom. 12:19, RSV).

It is significant in this connection that Paul does not deny the principle of vengeance. He realized that in this imperfect and violent world, human beings yearn for some kind of justice. When people have suffered at the hands of thieves and murderers, they usually hope that such evil will someday be overcome. To believe that the universe is as unfair as everyday experience is too demoralizing to tolerate. This may be one reason why the Judeo-Christian and Islamic religions have developed such elaborate systems of belief in the final judgment, when all accounts will be paid in full, both for good and ill. What Paul counsels in Romans is patient reliance on the instruments of divine justice.

The most significant question with regard to vengeance is what to do in the meanwhile. If people simply harbor their hatred and fail to express it, they sicken; if they give way to the desire for vengeance and take the law into their own hands, they usually suffer disastrous consequences. As the saying goes, "It costs more to avenge injuries than to bear them."[18] In place of zealous vigilantism, Paul advises two things: an active concern for the life and well-being of one's adversary and submission to lawful governmental authority. At first glance these appear to be flatly contradictory.

The concern for the good of one's enemies is dealt with first: "Instead, if your enemy is hungry, feed him; if he is thirsty, give him drink. For in so doing you heap coals of fire on his head"(Rom. 12:20). This verse specifies what was meant earlier in this chapter by the admonition, "Repay no one evil for evil"(Rom. 12:17). Whereas the natural tendency is to respond to violence with violence, to meanness with reprisals, the actions of mercy aim to break the deadly cycle. The abiding guideline of the church is the commitment to "overcome evil with good," as Romans 12:21 sets forth.

A convincing case has been made that the metaphor of burning charcoal on the head of adversaries depicts their repentance and remorse rather than painful vengeance against them.[19] The strategy Paul recommends seeks not only the well-being but also the transformation of persecutors and criminals. "Do not be overcome by evil, but overcome evil with good"(Rom. 12:21, RSV). This is not to say that what one aims to achieve will actually be accomplished in every instance. Those commentators who accuse Paul of being an incurable optimist in these verses confuse, in my opinion, intentions with results. As Paul knew from personal experience, there are some adversaries who react to being shamed by such unanticipated gestures of love by redoubling the intensity of their hatred. The question is what one aims to achieve: in the final analysis, not vengeance but transformation.

The other half of the counsel Paul offers is to submit to lawful authority. This is laid out in Romans 13:1-7, one of the most controversial passages in the Pauline epistles. Here Paul flatly states that those who resist governing authorities resist God. For the government serves as "the servant of God to execute God's wrath on the wrongdoer." The idea here is that a primary means of what *The Virginian* called "instruments of providence" is governmental law enforcement.

There were mitigating circumstances that help us understand why Paul was so positive in his appraisal of the Roman government. When Paul was writing Romans 13, an exemplary period of Roman justice and law enforcement was nearing its climax. The court system was being administered with unusual fairness; the conspiracy laws had been abolished; the emperor himself was obeying the law—which, given the fact that his name was Nero, and that within a few years he would turn into a paranoid who violated every law in the book, is worth mentioning. Paul did not foresee what was to come when he made the sweeping claims in this passage, and thus we are justified in taking his views with a grain or two of salt. When the law is perverted by a Marshal Stockburn, some form of resistance seems justified. Yet the most serious question this passage raises is whether it does not contradict the business of heaping coals on the head of one's enemy, of offering the enemy food and drink.

How could Paul have it both ways? How can he call upon the Christian community to pray for its enemies and bless those who persecute it, and at the same time urge obedience to the government, which "bears the sword" to execute divine wrath on criminals?

Paul's Holy Inconsistency

The common-sense answer is surely that Paul is inconsistent, that one or the other side of his position should be abandoned. This is what the Christian community has usually done. The law-and-order advocates have taken Romans 13:1–7 and have dropped the idea of loving the enemy. From the tradition of the divine right of kings to the proponents of submission to Adolf Hitler in Lutheran and Catholic Germany, the word has been to obey the emperor or the Führer as a kind of God. And as for the enemies, let them be rooted out, harassed, and destroyed.

Others in the Christian tradition have taken Romans 12 to heart and abandoned 13. They have urged the love of enemies no matter what their scale of provocation, no matter how many atrocities they may have committed. Those holding this preference have tended to oppose the use of law enforcement powers to punish criminals, to resist the use of war-making powers to curb the actions of tyrants.

I grant that either position has a kind of consistency that Paul seems to lack. But as I have mulled over this passage, I have found myself wondering whether there is not a deeper consistency of human experience that Paul is tapping in Romans 12 and 13. Look what has happened in our cultural tradition: having resisted strong law enforcement ever since our struggle against the British crown, we have tolerated remarkably high levels of violence and disorder. On the American frontier in the decades before *The Virginian* was written, for example, there was very lax law enforcement, little protection for the rights of the weak, and a series of economic disorders that proved destructive to stable relationships. Hundreds of vigilante actions occurred in response to those evils, some of them inspired by the religious heritage I sketched earlier. But vigilantism inevitably disguised what amounted to personal vengeance. The net result of such actions was the further erosion of security and a popularization of violence. Lacking a widely shared belief in the government as the agency of divine wrath against criminals, we found it necessary to invent "instruments of providence" in the form of frontiersmen, tall cowboys, and later superheroic figures.

The problem is that such superheroic stories serve to popularize the very antisocial behavior that causes much of the problem in the first place. I believe that the impact of such superheroic "disguises for vengeance" is visible not only in the unusually high crime statistics in the United States but also in the increasing frequency of mass murderers. The society influenced by these stories is facing a virtual epidemic of cool and relentless killers. Several years ago a colleague and I presented a paper on this topic, suggesting that recent assassins and mass murderers have tended to model their behavior after the avengers of the superheroic dramas.[20] They differ from "normal" citizens in the society in that they take the mythic paradigm of *The Virginian* seriously, tracking down persons they imagine are offenders and giving them vigilante justice, swift and direct.

These considerations lead me to wonder whether the seeming contradiction of Paul's perspective may not be superior to the tradition our culture has favored. If you abandon the idea of the government as the agent of divine wrath, then you shall have to invent such agents—which is precisely what our culture has done. People who are suffering from abuse and injustice simply will not tolerate a world in which there is no hope for tidying up the score. But to glorify the heroes of vigilante justice is to sow the seeds of our own destruction. It is to allow us to think that we might become vigilante heroes or heroines ourselves, or at least elect one in the marshal's office or the White House. When that happens, respect for the law disintegrates, and the yearning for violent resolution of the quick-and-easy sort gains highly dangerous, public forms.

Is there not perhaps a more healthy balance in Paul's view? A kind of holy inconsistency? Paul holds fast to the idea of divine vengeance, both in the world to come and in the form of vigorous law enforcement by a duly constituted government. But at the same time he strongly resists any involvement in vengeance on our own behalf: "Beloved, never avenge yourselves," because no one should ever attempt to become an impartial judge in her own cause. And to counter the poison of vengeance that afflicts anyone who is abused and persecuted, as the early Christians were, Paul counsels that "if your enemy is hungry, feed him; if he is thirsty, give him drink; for by doing this you will pile up burning coals upon his head."

Is there perhaps a deeper, more divine logic at work here? Are humans really capable of such actions if they are not entirely certain of the final judgment of God, the final triumph of righteousness? How can persecuted people counter despair without such a hope? How can they gain the power to respond creatively with burning coals except by trusting finally in the power of God either to transform or to punish the wicked? Is there not perhaps a deeper understanding of the human psyche in Paul's apparent inconsistency than in our cultural simplicities?

Two Concluding Suggestions

I leave these questions for you to ponder, because they are larger than I can comprehend on my own. Yet to take Paul's position seriously is to question certain aspects of our cultural tradition, to change our attitudes toward popular entertainment, and to alter our perspective on the proper role of government. It provokes us to think about what Roger Bacon wrote in his essays: "Revenge is a kind of wild justice; which the more man's nature runs to, the more ought law to weed it out."[21] Private vengeance disguised as selfless redemption has now reached such proportions in our society that we must begin to develop a new respect for the law, for equal but firm justice under law. This pondering leads to two practical suggestions.

The first relates to Paul's concern for an impartial system of law enforcement. Obviously, if we seek the perfection of the myths, we shall find any legal system fatally flawed; there were numerous loopholes in Paul's time as well. But when our system works fairly well, we should not stifle expressions of support and appreciation. When the Evanston police arrested mass murderer Alton Coleman, quickly, efficiently, and without undue use of force, we had every reason to be proud. We should find ways to express our gratitude when a system patterned on Paul's ideal of due process of law functions properly. And we should constantly be ready to support international institutions of this sort, comparable to the kind of international law enforcement that the Roman Empire offered when this letter was written.

Second, there is a need to develop contemporary ways to "pile up burning coals" on the heads of adversaries. While trusting in the final vengeance of God, whether in this life or the next, there is the practical task of feeding enemies and seeking the welfare of abusers. Rather than retaliating against neighbors, the challenge is find ways to help them. Rather than simply seeking the defeat of national adversaries, the challenge is to discover ways to assist them. This is not to condone their crimes or to diminish the injuries they have caused; if Paul is right, the crimes of our enemies and our own crimes will be avenged in God's good time, both in this world and the next. In the meanwhile, it makes sense to set about the business of seeking to overcome evil with good. Only in this way will it be possible truly to become instruments of God's peace. For "vengeance is mine, I will repay, says the Lord."

11

Works of Darkness
in *Red Dawn*

Besides this, knowing the time, that the hour [has] already
[come] for you to be awakened from sleep,
    for the salvation is closer to us now than when we first
    had faith.
The night is far gone,
    the day has drawn near.
Let us therefore put off the works of darkness
    but let us put on the armor of light.
Let us walk honorably as in [the] day,
    not in carousings and drunkenness,
        not in [sexual] affairs and indecencies,
            not in strife and jealousy,
but put on the Lord Jesus Christ
    and make no provision for the flesh [to gratify] its desires.
(Rom. 13:11–14)

In the work I have done over the last decade and a half to
relate biblical thought to American culture, the conviction
has gradually developed that highly popular films, television series, novels, and comics can serve as a kind of cultural barometer. This conviction was sustained by a 1985
issue of *Newsweek* in which Sylvester Stallone appeared on

the cover as Rocky, draped in the national flag. The cover article probed the reasons for the remarkable commercial success of *Rocky* and *Rambo*: "their deeper source was Stallone's own intuitive—or as some prefer, cynical—feel for the Zeitgeist. . . . He is filmmaker to a damn-mad blue-collar America that doesn't want to take it anymore."[1] The article concludes with the reflection that "Rocky and Rambo are figures of redemption . . . after the anti-heroics of the recent past, a trend in mass culture that reflected a nation's fallen regard for itself. Our fantasy heroes are less mirrors of what we are than windows into what we might like to be."[2]

The fact that so many films of this type have been popular in recent years leads one to take this idea of windows for national wish fulfillment with some seriousness. *Rocky IV, Invasion USA, Commando, Uncommon Valor, Missing in Action, The Terminator,* and *Red Dawn* should be studied as seriously as Siegfried Kracauer's analysis of German films of the 1920s and early '30s.[3] The wide popularity of these violent films involves a subtle interplay with the audience, revealing to some degree the taste and values of current Americans. These dramas of public redemption can serve to channel and legitimate aggressive impulses.

Red Dawn and the Night "Far Gone"

When I first read the reviews of *Red Dawn*,[4] I thought it might connect with Paul's words, "you know what hour it is. . . . [T]he night is far gone, the day is at hand. Let us then cast off the works of darkness and put on the armor of light" (Rom. 13:11–12, RSV). The film is set in an American town in the West at the beginning of World War III. News headlines tell of Greens gaining control in Germany, of Mexico in revolution, and NATO dissolving. The United States stands alone. The scene shifts to a beautiful mountain scene, then to a quiet Western town with typical clapboard houses, and kids going to school. A group of high school fellows discuss having lost a football game as they head off to class. The history teacher looks out of the window and is astonished to see paratroopers landing. Cuban and Nicaraguan troops with their Russian advisers begin to impose a totalitarian reign of terror. Members of the high school football team, "the Wolverines," embark on a guerrilla campaign whose courage and audacity inspires a resurgence of national pride that helps to save the country.

In a significant scene at the beginning of the movie, the young guerrillas are wondering how they can survive without grocery stores and the comfort of their families. Daryl, the student body president, says, "As Calumet student body president, I forward the motion that we give ourselves up." One of the other fellows says, "I second the motion, we can't sit here, we need stuff, and . . ." Jed, the natural leader of the group who had already graduated from high school, says to the seconder, "Sit down, Danny. You aren't going anywhere; it's too dangerous to go into town." The student body president responds, "I say we vote on it." "There isn't going to be any vote," Jed replies. He and the student body leader scuffle, and the latter is knocked down. The self-elected leader tells the other fellows to walk out if they want. This has to be a John Wayne operation, with an endowed superleader. As the film develops, Daryl, the student body president who advocates the democratic procedure, ends up being the traitor who sells out to the Russians.

The film provides an opportunity to reflect on two patterns of behavior that are vying for the mind of contemporary Americans—zealous nationalism and prophetic realism. I think these opposing ideologies can be linked with Paul's view of the conflict between the old age and the new. The old age of *Red Dawn* celebrates regeneration through violence at the hands of superheroic leaders who disdain democratic methods. It is true to the Orwellian vision of *1984* in which adversaries become mirror images of each other, both using totalitarian means to defend values and institutions. The new age that Paul describes, on the other hand, celebrates Christ for having defeated the principalities and powers, setting the oppressed and the deluded free from destructive patterns of behavior.

My plan to investigate the link between Romans and *Red Dawn* was foiled when the film stopped playing in the Chicago area before I had a chance to view it. So the best I could do when I first spoke on this theme was to report seeing an odd form of dawn. Early one morning as we were driving back toward Chicago from the west I saw a false dawn. While it was still quite dark, some color appeared toward the south, and I thought my sense of direction must have suddenly gone haywire, that Interstate 80 had suddenly veered off toward Canada. My mind was set at rest when the sky grew dark again. Then a few minutes later fingers of rosy light began to appear in the eastern sky. The night was far gone. This time, the day was at hand. I was reminded again of the line from Paul's letter to the Romans: So put "off the works of darkness and put on the armor of light!" (Rom. 13:12, RSV).

Later I was able to study a videotape of the film and reflect on the relationship with the details of Paul's admonition.

"Carousing and Drunkenness"

Paul's words in Romans represent an effort to grapple with the theme in *Red Dawn*: how to come to terms with the powerful myths and symbols of mass culture. As a leader in a small sectarian movement striving to retain a distinct identity over against a corrupt and violent world, Paul names some of the works of darkness that were particularly popular in the Rome to which this letter was addressed: "let us conduct ourselves becomingly as in the day, not in reveling and drunkenness" (Rom. 13:13, RSV). This first pair of works of darkness convey a life pattern of self-destruction. Both terms are in the plural, suggesting "frequent repetition."[5] The term translated here as "reveling," or better, "carousings," originally was used to depict the "festal procession in honor of Dionysus"[6] or a joyous banquet, but in the New Testament it is always used in the negative sense of irresponsible carousing. A loss of self-control is typical for carousings and drunken bouts. One seeks to escape from responsibilities or troubles into a state of wild abandon and drugged insensibility.

Today we might classify this form of behavior as escapist, and there are many who feel that escapism is pretty harmless. A similar attitude was evident in the Rome of the first century, where carousings and drunken stupors were typical of the rich as well as the poor. The film *I, Claudius,* gives some sense of the vicious scope of such debased behavior among the ruling elite, which was emulated on a less expensive scale by the urban poor.

Paul disagreed that escapism is harmless. He was convinced that the wrath was coming, and that it was already visible in the self-destructive behavior of the old age. "For salvation is nearer to us now than when we first believed; the night is far gone, the day is at hand" (Rom. 13:11–12, RSV). A society or an individual hooked on escapist patterns of behavior is likely to self-destruct. One day the roof falls in, the term is up, the grades are reported. People wake up after the last in a series of drunken parties to discover that they have lost out on life, that they have passed the point of no return, and that the disaster is upon them. *Red Dawn* apparently had something like this in mind, when a nation obsessed with its gadgets, junk foods, and football games suddenly finds itself mortally threatened and discovers that the will to cope is gone—except of course for the Wolverines! Which is another escapist fantasy in itself!

But it does not require a story like that in *Red Dawn* to explain what Paul had in mind. Nations that have been drifting along with escapist fantasies suddenly find themselves facing financial chaos, or unmanageable famine, or social disintegration, or a catastrophic war that comes through sloth and misjudgment. The causes of the old world order cannot be externalized and projected onto evil conspiracies; they are endemic in the human condition and thus the responsibility of everyone. ". . . the night is far gone. . . . Let us then cast off the works of darkness . . ."

"Debauchery and Licentiousness"

The second pair of works of darkness that Paul names in our text is "debauchery and licentiousness." The first word is literally "beddings," which implies sleeping around, having sexual intercourse with anyone who happens to be available. The second word, also in the plural, is closer to the term "debaucheries" or "sensualities." It connotes behavior that experiments with sensations, lacking internal moral standards that might set any limits. Bedding on impulse and seeking sensual excitement fit in the category of exploitative behavior—using others for one's own pleasure, regardless of consequences. And again, in the Rome of the first century, such sexual exploitation was generally viewed as harmless. A few moralists inveighed against the sexual depravities of a Claudius and a Nero and their associates, and despised prophets from the Jewish or Christian traditions issued warnings about the wrath of God, but what Paul calls the "works of darkness" were among the most popular and widely discussed activities of the age.

There is little need to point out the similarities in popular attitudes today. I recently read a telling statistic: percentage of sexual acts on television between married partners—7; percentage between unmarried partners—93. The most popular forms of entertainment convey the view of sexual license as harmless, while other media such as pornographic films, videotapes, and printed materials depict every form of sexual experimentation. *Red Dawn* does not fall into the sexually exploitative category; the only elements of abuse are performed by the Russians, whose victims later join the Wolverines to gain revenge. The theme of sexual distortion is more fully developed in a film like *Rambo*. Until Rambo met a tough resistance fighter, the beautiful Co, he "couldn't bear even the thought of getting that close to someone. Not just emotionally. Literally. Physically. . . . Because when you got that near to someone you were unprotected, vulnerable. Because during sex you lost control."[7] After they consummate a brief moment of love, Co is killed. The story remains true to the paradigm in which superheroic figures remain separate and alone, never losing control.[8] So Rambo does not have to modify his super independence by taking on the burdens of a permanent relationship.

Perhaps in light of recent experience, it sounds less moralistic than it once did to affirm Paul's view that sexual exploitation is wrong. There is, in fact, an underlying connection between such exploitation and superheroic independence. The underlying issue is sexual gratification without union, without fidelity to a partner. And an impartial view of what is happening to children and to the weak in American society today would confirm Paul's classification of such exploitation, no matter how heroic it may sometimes appear, as among "the works of darkness." To lower the moral barriers against random sexual inclinations is to open the door to more serious forms of exploitation: rape, incest, brutalization, and murder. America is facing a mounting tide of sexual evil: children who have suffered from parental bed swapping and from sexual exploitation themselves are turning their rage and demoralization on others, in ever more destructive forms. Who can look within without recognizing the tendency to condone and to participate in some of these "works of darkness"? Has there been much honest debate, moving beyond petty moralism, on the social and personal consequences of debauchery? "The night is far gone, the day is at hand," Paul writes. "Let us then cast off the works of darkness and put on the armor of light!"

"Quarreling and Jealousy"

The final pair of "works of darkness" that Paul lists is much more straightforward in translation: "quarreling and jealousy." These are the expression of what one might call the principle of domination. The desire to be number one results in endless quarreling, and the envy of those who are ahead is what Paul calls "jealousy." The one is typical of those who aspire to dominate; the other is typical of those who have failed to dominate. The will to dominate thus lies at the root of both quarreling and jealousy.

In the class-bound and highly competitive society of the Greco-Roman world, these traits were widely expressed and generally accepted. The personality type characteristic of the Mediterranean world of the first century was oriented to public recognition and status.[9] People's sense of self-identity was largely dependent on the admiration of others. To "be somebody" meant that you had to be ahead of someone, capable of evoking their jealousy. The social world in which the early church found itself was marked by chronic forms of squabbling and envy, which were thought to be the natural form of social relations. Social domination was simply assumed.

There are increasing signs that American society is moving in the same direction. The rich are getting richer and the poor poorer, the tradition of democratic equality is weakening, and the admiration of the great and powerful, always a factor in our society, seems to be growing stronger. "Dallas" and "Falconcrest" were among the most popular prime-time television programs in recent decades, involving millions of lower- and middle-class people in enjoying and vicariously participating in the quarreling and jealousy of the super rich. The appeal of domination seems at times to be as strong within religious institutions as it is outside of them, with leaders vying for prestigious positions while drifting into destructive patterns of envy and abuse. There are times when passionate arguments about theology or policy or strategy are disguised expressions of the will to dominate, when jealousy of those who get more attention or higher grades or more recognition from superiors is the reverse side of that same brutal will to be on top.

What I particularly wanted to explore in *Red Dawn* was the explicit repudiation of egalitarian standards on the part of the heroic young people who fight against the paratroopers. One of the ominous features of a society dominated by superheroic myths is that equality and democratic processes fall increasingly into disrepute. In the film, the advocate of democratic process and his father the mayor are stereotyped as traitors to American principles. Not only does the mayor collaborate with the invaders, tipping them off about families that might make trouble, but in the end he turns in his own son, who had been a member of the Wolverine partisans. Daryl is forced to swallow a direction signal that the paratroopers can follow up to the snowbound mountain hideout. In the gun battle that follows, the Reds are repulsed but the electronic direction finder is discovered, and Daryl along with a Russian prisoner are shot by Jed and the most fanatical of the Wolverines. Remorseless methods of domination are therefore presented in this film as the proper means of saving an egalitarian society.

Just before the execution, one of the reluctant Wolverines asks about the rules of war. The zealous leader replies, "I never heard of the Geneva Convention." Another boy queries, "What then is the difference between us and them?" The Wolverines had witnessed mass executions by Reds in reprisal raids. Jed replies that the difference is "because we live here." In the context of the film, this answer suffices. But in the process, the mirror image effect of *1984* comes to light: by defending democratic institutions against totalitarian foes with totalitarian means, American culture becomes more totalitarian itself.

Films like *Red Dawn* should be identified by their proper names. They provide propaganda for a false dawn. Their methods and values are those of the night, not the day. And when nations follow such values, they bring darkness upon themselves. Movie critic David Denby plunged into debate with popular culture when he labeled *Rambo* and *Red Dawn* "fascist films." "It's possible," Denby argued, that "we're seeing the stirrings of incipient fascism—a distant American variant combining paranoia, military fantasy, and a style of individualism so extreme as to be pathological."[10] In a penetrating article titled "Fascist Guns," J. Hoberman concludes that "perhaps the most fascistic aspect" of these films is their "faith in the regenerative . . . powers of war. The very title 'Red Dawn' implies a rebirth."[11] The striking parallels to earlier forms of European fascism are visible in J. W. Scott's recent discussion of the connection between "authoritarianism and individual heroic action." Fascist "shock troops refer to themselves as bands of patriotic knights, soldiers and warriors, willing to kill, if not die, for their version of the nation. Georges Valois wrote that 'the Best, the Strongest, are first of all men capable of violent struggle. The strongest individual is the warrior capable of establishing peace so that work can be carried out.'"[12]

Mythic reenactments of regeneration through violence such as *Red Dawn* should be recognized as containing lethal means of deluding leaders and nations, encouraging them to act in destructive, imprudent ways. Fortunately, *Red Dawn* is so "virulently alarmist" and "dementedly feverish" that it lacks the power to convince audiences to emulate its actions.[13] But it would be well for Americans to walk carefully, because there are twentieth-century examples of people who follow the mythic logic of fascism into disaster. It also happened to Rome in A.D. 62, a few years after Paul wrote these words in Romans, when Nero finally succumbed to the totalitarian logic implicit in his escapism, his exploitative sexual behavior, and his illusions of divinity. The empire turned paranoid and began devouring innocent victims by summary executions and persecutions of scapegoats. It is likely that Paul was one of the victims of this process of imperial self-destruction. Individuals as well as nations pay a high price when those in power succumb to false dawns that glorify the "works of darkness."

Defenses Against a False Dawn

In this passage Paul was appealing for the members of the church in Rome to beware of false dawns, so to speak, and to make sure that their pattern of life was consistent with the real dawn of Christ's reign. "Besides this, you know what hour it is, how it is full time now for you to wake from sleep. For salvation is nearer to us now than when we first believed; the night is far gone, the day is at hand." Many persons in the current decade have had a similarly uncanny sense that darkness is upon us again with full force. Escapism, exploitation, and domination seem to have won the day. Some of the most popular entertainments today are those with a fascist ideology of total darkness, disguised as light. And if the nation continues to act out the mythic plot of regeneration through violence, the consequences could be disastrous for all. What Paul sensed for his time may be true for ours as well: that the night is far gone and a day of judgment is at hand.

The great temptation in such a time is to use the "works of darkness" to struggle against the darkness that surrounds us. *Red Dawn* places this temptation in highly alluring form. A reviewer in *Christianity Today* touts the "nobility of spirit" promoted by the film.[14] But I contend that the better alternative is to put on what Paul called "the armor of light." This metaphor is drawn from the apocalyptic depictions of the coming war between the forces of light and of darkness, implying active struggle against evil.[15] In our humane religious and intellectual heritage, there are sufficient resources to ward off the false dawn of popular entertainments that can lure the country into self-destruction. There remains a legacy of common sense and commitment to democratic processes that could be employed to make wiser choices, both about the forms of entertainment that Americans will support and about the kinds of policies they will pay for. America may well go through a lot of darkness in the years ahead, but there is no need for persons of faith to carry midnight along the way. To wear the "armor of light" is to be realistic about the dangers of the "works of darkness," and to renounce them—over and over again. In Paul's view, to wear the "armor of light" is to wake up from escapism and mind-numbing addictions. It is to replace sexual and personal exploitation with righteous relationships in which the blessings of God can prosper and the young and the immature can be nurtured. To wear the "armor of light" means that there is no further need for domination; instead of quarreling and envy there will be strength for cooperation and the mutual facing of the challenges that lie ahead.

Paul goes on to admonish the Roman Christians to "put on the Lord Jesus Christ" (Rom. 13:14). This reference to Jesus leads me to make a final critical assessment about films like *Red Dawn* and *Rambo*. Jesus remains a tragic figure; he proved vulnerable to death. And he died, not slaying others, but taking the place on the cross that should have been occupied by a forerunner of Jed and Rambo, a zealot revolutionary by the name of Barabbas. This model of self-sacrificing death has long influenced the taste of Western culture. Until the rise in the 1930s of the American monomyth where the superhero always wins, even popular forms of entertainment preferred stories where the hero tragically dies. This tragic legacy is reflected in a broad stream of the cultural inheritance in American society. The biblical heritage reminds us in the words of the psalmist, "Some boast of chariots, and some of horses, but we boast of the name of Yahweh our God. They will collapse and fall; but we shall rise and stand upright" (Ps. 20:7–8). Great literature and film point in the same direction, showing the tragic consequences of boasting of superheroic chariots and horses.

Red Dawn retains an element of this classic paradigm, because the leader of the Wolverines falls in battle after sending two survivors back to tell the tale. He bleeds to death on a park bench, tenderly holding a mortally wounded member of his band. This tragic ending did not endear itself to viewers, and made it a much less popular film than *Rambo: First*

Blood, where the superhero wins against incredible odds and returns to savor his victory, bloody but unbowed. On these grounds I would rate *Red Dawn* higher than *Rambo*. There is a need for realism about the price of regeneration through violence.

Paul goes on in Romans 13:14 to urge Christians to "make no provision for the flesh, to gratify its desires." In this context, "flesh" implies both human potential and the demonic power of the old age itself.[16] The myths and institutions of a fallen world have the capacity of leading people to trust their presumably superior capacities in gaining what they desire. Superheroic myths in particular feed the narcissistic yearnings of individuals and nations to get whatever they want no matter what the limiting circumstances may be. If one is really super, then no dangers need be taken into account. But this ultimate form of depending on the "flesh," contrary to the superheroic films, is actually corrosive to genuine courage. This is the significance of a ludicrous episode involving Sylvester Stallone and the 1986 Cannes Film Festival. After the raid on Libya, which many observers aptly identified as an expression of "Ramboism," the creator of the Rambo films decided to cancel his attendance, "citing concern over terrorist attacks."[17] The irony was not lost on reporters who later observed Stallone, along with his wife, Brigitte Nielsen, and his burly bodyguards, shoving "their way up to the front of the line in a Georgetown ice cream parlor so that Sly and his bride could get their cones first. Rambo may not be much for European terrorists, but he'll do anything for double-dip chocolate chip."[18] These incidents, though insignificant in and of themselves, reveal something about the way superheroic myths place the "desires of the flesh" in a false and alluring form. While encouraging historical cowardice on the understandable premise that only those who are actually invulnerable can afford to take risks, superheroic stories lead people to violate democratic standards of fairness in getting whatever they desire when no countervailing force is visible.

In contrast to these fantasies of the night, the basic message that Paul conveys is that the Christian community should not conform to these mythic expectations. Believers are not called to fight the fire of the old age with an equally self-destructive fire. Christ died to expose the false dawn. It follows that to put on Christ is to renounce the nationalistic myths of regeneration through violence, of the domination of the strong over the weak. In the American setting, this involves renouncing and criticizing certain forms of mass entertainment that embody those myths, luring viewers to pattern their behavior after the models of their superheroes. "The night is far gone. The day has drawn near. Let us therefore put off the works of darkness but let us put on the armor of light!"

12

Epilogue: "Saint" Paul and *Dead Poets Society*

I thank God whom I serve out of the ancestral tradition with a clear conscience, as I remember you ceaselessly in my prayers night and day; remembering your tears, I desire to see you that I might be filled with joy, recalling your sincere faith, which dwelt first in your grandmother Lois and your mother Eunice and now, I am confident, dwells also in you. Therefore I remind you to reignite the charisma of God that is in you through the laying on of my hands. For God did not give us a spirit of timidity, but of power and love and self-restraint.

(2 Tim. 1:3–7)

Second Timothy was probably written forty or fifty years after Paul's death in an effort to deal with the situation this book has had to confront from the start.[1] How can the Pauline gospel be appropriated in a time and place far removed from his original ministry? How can his legacy be recaptured after suffering misuse and misinterpretation, albeit with the best of intentions on the part of traditional interpreters? Should we have nerve enough to relate this legacy to the powerful movies that are shaping the outlook of our day? The text of 2 Timothy 1:3–7 deals with the force of ancestral tradition and the reigniting of the charisma received from God. Both themes have relevance to the movie, *Dead Poets Society*,[2] which grapples with an issue similar to the one we face in Pauline studies.

The "Dead Poets Society" was established by teenaged students at the exclusive Welton Academy in New England. The boys are being molded by parents and a stiffly legalistic school staff, loyal to the ideals of "Tradition," "Honor," "Discipline," and "Excellence."[3] They are captivated by a charismatic poetry teacher, John Keating, played by Robin Williams, who teaches them the gift of the inspired word. The fellows discover that Keating had formed a Dead Poets Society when he was a student in Welton, memorizing and declaiming romantic poetry in secret meetings held in a cave down by the river. So seven boys in the class of 1959 decide to emulate their teacher. They sneak out at night and begin to discover their own voices. In time they overcome their timidity. Their ringleader, Neil Perry, defies his stern father and takes the role of Puck in a performance of the Shakespearean play. He turns out to be a wonderful performer, and declares that "acting is everything to me."[4] When his father decides to remove him from the subversive influence of the poetry teacher by sending him to a military academy, Neil commits suicide. Keating is fired and the Dead Poets Society is disbanded.

Is there a deeper meaning to this story to which the text from 2 Timothy may provide access? Must the conflict between ancestral tradition and charismatic gifts always require so high a price? Is it appropriate to consider those of us who are attempting to reinterpret Paul in response to contemporary culture as a kind of Dead Poets Society?

The Dilemma of Ancestral Faith

Second Timothy, along with the other pastoral epistles, gives particular emphasis to the Jewish roots of Christianity. We encounter this in the very first line of the scripture that opens this chapter, in an expression that is very hard to translate into English. Literally, Paul says he serves God "from ancestors"—not from fathers alone.[5] Finding no English expression available, I translate this as serving "out of the ancestral tradition." Paul's service to God is here seen in complete continuity with his Jewish roots. In one Bible commentator's words, the Paul of 2 Timothy "did not view Christianity as an abrupt departure from the religion of his forbearers, but rather its fulfillment and development."[6]

The second letter to Timothy suggests that nothing about Paul's conversion changed his devotion to ancestral tradition in any way. Paul's break with the Jewish law and his silence about his parents in the authentic letters are overlooked here.[7] The contrast with an authentic Pauline passage like Philippians 3:3–7 is particularly stark. This "Hebrew born of Hebrews," formerly proud of his lineage from the tribe of Benjamin, says he counted it all as loss for the sake of Christ. But in 2 Timothy, the voice of Paul is made to say that he served God according to his ancestral legacy, "with a clear conscience." The entire issue of Paul's discovery of his own bad faith in persecuting the early church for violating ancestral tradition is here set aside. The Paul of history is here being absorbed into a new persona, what we subsequently call "Saint" Paul.

The language of verse 5 is even more striking, because it refers to the maternal tradition that had shaped Timothy. His "sincere" faith dwelled "first in your grandmother Lois and your mother Eunice." Timothy's mother is mentioned in Acts 16:1 as being a Christian "believer" when young Timothy entered Paul's service. But to extend the legacy back to his grandmother Lois is to reaffirm once again the Hebraic roots. Genuine faith is here defined as traditional Jewish faith. It is also intriguing, given the generally negative attitude of the pastorals toward the role of women,[8] to find Timothy's early life so completely defined by a maternal legacy.[9] But of course the basic premise of 2 Timothy is that Paul, the elder male apostle, passes on the precious legacy to the younger male, Timothy. Paul is the ultimate authority figure in 2 Timothy; he is now a "saint," devoid of the foibles and weaknesses that had marked his actual ministry. Saintliness here—and in the tradition of Welton Academy—seems to imply a form of truth that one should not question and a form of behavior that consists of obedience to authority.

The premise of a saintly and unchallengeable tradition is what marks Welton Academy in this Peter Weir film. In the opening scene of the movie, the headmaster reminds everyone in a chapel service that, just as the boys light their candles from the flame held by an older teacher, so the "light of knowledge shall be passed from old to young."[10] The headmaster of the academy is furious at any breach of obedience, any sign of nonconformity. But the problem with such a saintly, ancestral tradition is made manifest in *Dead Poets Society*. The headmaster admonishes Keating at one point not to lead his students into the independence promoted by the great poets. "Prepare them for college," he urges, "and the rest will take care of itself." But the contrary voice of John Keating remains much more compelling: "I always thought education was learning to think for yourself."[11] One might even say that the clash between the poetic impulse and the ancestral tradition provoked the disaster in the story.

From the perspective of radical Pauline theology, a similar problem emerges. To link faith so completely with ancestral tradition, whether Jewish or Christian, whether maternal or paternal, diminishes the revolutionary power of faith. Faith in the Pauline sense calls for a thorough transformation of ancestral patterns; faith overturns parental expectations. Faith in Christ means loyalty to the one crucified by society, repudiated by parents, rejected by the ancestral religion, denied by the Jewish culture. The authentic Paul stands close to the saying of Jesus: "If anyone comes to me and does not hate his own father and mother . . . he cannot be my disciple" (Luke 14:26, RSV). The film stands closer to Paul and Jesus on this point than does 2 Timothy. It encourages us in the endeavor to set Paul free to become the apostle to America.

Yet *Dead Poets Society* shows the terrible price of allowing a split between parents and poets, between tradition and inspiration, to remain unresolved. Was the suicidal ending of the story really inevitable? Should the poets always force people into deadly crises with their tradition? their ancestors? their churches? Are we forced into an intractable conflict with the traditional view of Paul?

This basic issue is one that 2 Timothy sought to address. The writer of the pastorals made a valiant effort to retain both sides: the Pauline gospel and the Jewish roots. There was a desperate need for such balance during the late first century. The attitude taken by 2 Timothy stands between two extremes in family relations that marked the church around the end of the first century. On the right wing of the Pauline churches, so to speak, there was the apocalyptic radicalism of the ascetic Thekla group.[12] On the left wing were the Gnostic circles of intellectuals.[13] Both sides rejected parental tradition and bodily responsibility. Both repudiated on principle the tasks of parenting and cultural maintenance. The film presents a parallel attitude by stereotyping all the parents of Welton students as uptight villains. They appear as the villains set against the pure white light of the poets.[14] Would that it were really so simple!

The issue of ancestral faith is also crucial for the reinterpretation of Paul and his letters for the contemporary American context. The second letter to Timothy causes us to wonder whether authentic interpretation requires attention to both sides: the absorption of ancestral values shaped by tradition and the transforming power of the poetry, the gospel. The tension between these two sides may in fact be a key to the vitality of responsible hermeneutics. Perhaps we should think of current interpreters as a kind of dead poets society, in which the inspired "saints" of the past play the role of the dead poets. Yet we are called to live in critical interaction with that past; we are constantly challenged to evaluate our ancestral religion and its interpretation of scripture. The same critical spirit should guide our interpretation of movies, no matter how popular and appealing they may be. This book is a pilgrimage that moves along the border between tradition, on the one side, and the revolutionary power of the cross and the spirit, on the other. This trajectory brings me face to face with a nerve center of popular imagination and insight as embodied in the movies. But neither with regard to my interpretation of Pauline texts nor contemporary films can I ever be fully satisfied, ever fully at ease. If the internal tensions were eliminated, the interpreter's balance wheel would no longer be functional.

Reigniting the Gift

The second half of the text from 2 Timothy deals with rekindling or reigniting the charisma received from God. The term "charisma" is defined as the Spirit, according to verse 7. Paul had taught that each member of the church receives a gift of the spirit. The pastoral epistles narrow this down to the charisma given to leaders who stand in the apostolic succession.[15] In the words of 2 Timothy, it is the "charisma of God that is in you through the laying on of my hands." The focus here is on the ordained ministry, not the ministry of the church as a whole. Before he became "Saint" Paul in the generation after his death, Paul's view of the gifts of the spirit included the talents of all members of the early Christian congregations. If Paul were living today, it would even include the gift to interpret the movies that many movie lovers possess. But even though I would prefer the more democratic orientation of the authentic Pauline letters, the message of 2 Timothy makes a useful point. The gift needs to be reignited. The fire will die out without care. It falters when not fueled.

I had an intriguing reminder of the necessity of maintenance on the way home from seeing *Dead Poets Society* with a group of seminary students. Sometime between 11:30 and midnight my old car picked up what our text calls "a spirit of timidity." We stalled on a corner without a garage in sight. The nearest shelter and telephone were in a yuppie bar, which struck some of our colleagues as pretty funny. But they could hardly believe the report I later received about the part that needed replacement. It was the igniter!

An igniter can wear out, I discovered. For thousands of miles it faithfully conveyed power to the spark plugs. But when it began to wear down, the motor got timid in the middle of the street. "Reignite the charisma that is within you," says 2 Timothy. It will not sustain itself for ever. To see what is required in such rekindling requires the resources of the larger Pauline tradition as embodied in a Christian educational institution like the Welton Academy. The four school banners solemnly carried into the chapel at the opening convocation could have been drawn from the Pauline tradition as a whole and used in this book as a framework for understanding Pauline theology: "tradition, honor, discipline, excellence."

"Tradition" is what the pastoral epistles promote above all, as we have seen. The charismatic gifts received by leaders in the church have roots that need to be nourished, channels that provide directions and limits. These letters were written at a time when many churches were being led astray by charismatics and intellectuals who thought of themselves as divine and self-sufficient. The pastorals are intended to help anchor the church within the tradition, to find its identity in the story of faith. To absorb such a tradition is to follow the apostles, saints, and martyrs. Their lives give proof of what Keating argued in the poetry class at Welton Academy: "that words and ideas can change the world."[16] But the transforming quality of such ideas was hardly in view for the Academy as a whole any more than it was for the authors of the pastorals. When the headmaster asks one of the boys for a definition of "tradition," he is pleased to hear the response: "Tradition, Mr. Nolan, is the love of school, country, and family. Our tradition at Welton is to be the best!"[17] The competitive framework of these static ideals remains final: "our tradition" is superior to that of any other academy. This is sadly reminiscent of what has happened to Pauline theology in much of the traditional scope of interpretation. Our hope is related to Keating's vision, that the culturally transforming message of Paul might be set free from the weight of its traditional reformulation and related in powerful new ways to an imaginative stream of American culture.

"Honor" in the Welton Academy was defined in stilted, traditional terms as "dignity and the fulfillment of duty."[18] In contrast, the authentic strand of Pauline theology centers its attention on the ultimate source of honor and the root cause of its corruption. It recognizes God as the source of honor; igniters are not created by themselves. They are designed and created by the manufacturer. Hence the central human dilemma, as we have seen in the Pauline letters, is to recognize God as ultimate. Humans fall into dishonor, according to Romans (1:18–32), when they fail to honor God as God. They become twisted and pathological. But properly honoring God also means honoring the gifts people have received, which is the crucial issue in *Dead Poets Society*. The twin threats of superiority and inferiority that Paul struggled against in 1 Corinthians 12:14–26 involve keeping charismatic gifts in perspective. The crucial task of human maturation, both for the students at Welton Academy and for the rest of us, is to discover how to integrate honor with love.

"Discipline" in the Welton Academy was largely a matter of accepting the authority of teachers and parents. As one honor student defined it for the headmaster at the beginning of the film, "Discipline is respect for parents, teachers, and headmaster."[19] In the authentic Pauline letters, this kind of authoritarian discipline is replaced by the kind of self-discipline that is required to keep the flame ignited. This is a major emphasis in Romans 12: "Never flag in zeal! Be aglow in the spirit! . . . Be constant in prayer!" (Rom. 12:11–12). "Pray without ceasing!" Paul urges in 1 Thessalonians (5:17). In Galatians he urges spiritual discipline: "If we live by the spirit, let us also walk by the spirit!" (5:25). There are numerous references in Paul's letters to his hard work and to the work of the congregation. He knew that the gift of the spirit must be maintained, nourished, allowed to grow. Work needs to alternate with worship and recreation if faith is to remain healthy. The apocalyptic urgency in Pauline theology that we have repeatedly discussed could properly be expressed by following the Latin motto employed in the film: *carpe diem!* The crucial discipline is to "seize the day." For sloth would allow the gift to die out.

"Tradition, honor, discipline," and finally . . . "excellence" are required to nourish the charisma the world has been given in the Pauline legacy. Gifts must be honed and practiced if they are to mature to effectiveness. And although the quest for excellence in scholarship is often perverted by the desire for success, as it was in Welton Academy,[20] it nevertheless remains essential. A truer expression was in the soccer games that John Keating coached in the film. In sports, he said, each person pits himself against others to achieve excellence. The exhilarating sports scenes in the film convey this deep educational need. The Pauline expression of this legacy is on the seal of the university where I teach: "whatsoever is true, whatsoever is excellent . . . think on these things!" (Phil. 4:8).

Yes, 2 Timothy is right in teaching that the charisma of God needs to be rekindled. It will not take care of itself. Everyone needs the admonition to keep it alive, to seize the day, to keep that igniter firing away, even in older-model vehicles of the senior-citizen type! It is a challenge that is relevant not only for the task of reinterpreting the Pauline legacy but also for living it out in the twenty-first century.

"Power and Love and Self-Restraint"

The second letter to Timothy goes on to describe the nature of the charisma itself, with words that resonate with the film. "For God did not give us a spirit of timidity, but of power," the author writes. He wanted leaders of Pauline churches, like Timothy, to take the authority of the tradition and use it boldly in the controversy with heretics. The spirit, he believed, should encourage leaders in assertiveness. And although we all know that assertive power can easily become abusive, there is a greater risk in its denial.

Timidity is the refusal to recognize and be responsible for our powers. It is the key educational hindrance in the film, which shows insecure boys saying "Yes, sir, I'm sorry" to their parents and teachers. They live in a chronic state of timidity. One of the seven members of the Dead Poets Society, Todd Anderson, is particularly timid. He fears his own voice and is reluctant to speak in public. He joins the Dead Poets Society only on the condition that he doesn't have to speak. But in the poetry class run by John Keating, such evasive timidity is not allowed. After writing and destroying countless beginnings of a poem to be composed and read to the class, Todd tells Keating that he doesn't have anything to recite. Keating brings him up to the front of the class and demands that he utter and then shout the barbaric "Yawp" mentioned in Walt Whitman's poem. Then he covers the boy's eyes and forces him to describe Whitman's picture in his own words until suddenly, a lyrical flow of words begins to erupt. The boy who thinks he has nothing to say turns out to be the one genuine poet in the class.

The greatest betrayal of charisma is timidity, if 2 Timothy is correct. It is the toughest barrier we have to cross in carrying forward an American view of Paul: compared with the great theologians and inspired preachers of the European and American past and present, who are we to speak? to think? to decide? to discern? When we face the daunting tasks of interpretation, the innovative challenge of the task encourages us to cower and seek a safe corner. Some interpreters conduct their entire careers in the spirit of timidity, using the well-tested words and ideas formed in another cultural tradition and for another situation. They never learn to trust their own gifts enough to exercise them so as to interact with their own cultural situation in the now. They are like the marchers in *Dead Poets Society* who naturally fall into step with one another, evoking the clapping of the crowd, which allows Keating to explain the threat to individualism:

> What it demonstrates is how difficult it is for any of us to listen to our own voice or maintain our own beliefs in the presence of others. If any of you think you would have marched differently, then ask yourself why you were clapping. Lads, there is a great need in all of us to be accepted, but you must trust what is unique or different about yourself, even if it is odd or unpopular.[21]

Without the courage to trust one's voice and charisma, the challenge of relating these Pauline texts to the issues and artifacts of our own culture can therefore scarcely be addressed. A great company of contemporary interpreters needs to heed the admonition, "seize the day!" For we have been given a spirit not of timidity but of power.

Yet power itself cannot be the last word. Second Timothy speaks of the spirit "of power and love." The mark of some of the leaders whom the pastoral epistles opposed was lovelessness, even the tendency to exploit. The issue is fundamental for interpreters in every age. Power without a responsible form of love can too easily become a power trip. There was an impressive expression of power in Neil's charismatic performance of the role of Puck. The movie shows him enjoying his appeal to the women in the cast as he impishly repeats the lines that epitomize the problematic link between love and power: "Cupid is a knavish lad, Thus to make poor females mad."[22] Like Neil, we interpreters can take such pleasure from the exercise of our charisma that its purpose may be perverted. There is a performance aspect of interpretation that can be irresistibly corrupting. As we lead or speak or counsel, the pleasures of rapt attention are often so great that we lose our perspective. We love the accolades at the end of the sermon or lecture, the compliments at the end of the successful solo performance, the honors and success that come to effective leaders. But power without love is destructive. It corrodes the charisma.

The final word of our text is this: "not . . . a spirit of timidity, but of power and love and self-restraint." If power needs the channeling of love, it also requires the resources of restraint. The usual translation of this philosophical and moral category (*sôphronismos*) is "self-control," but in fact no single English term does justice to the profound resonance this term had in the ancient world. It was used to teach people a due sense of limits, a recognition that no matter how powerful their gifts, they are not gods and goddesses, as we saw in the discussion of the necessary death of innocence in Romans 12:3. A lack of restraint leads inevitably to disaster in the ancient Greek tragedies. The term is related to sober-mindedness and moderation, the taste for the golden mean, for balance. A sound education seeks to instill and nurture such a taste, as important to the philosophers of the ancient world as it was to the author of 2 Timothy.

The tragedy of *Dead Poets Society* was directly related to a lack of restraint. Charles Perry abused his power as parent by trying to force his artistic son into a profession promising wealth and status. But his son Neil also showed a fatal lack of restraint. His wildly successful performance in the play provided such a sense of his own powers that he could not bear the thought of their restraint. In the restrictive realm of his parent's home on the night of his triumphant performance, Neil placed on his head the crown of thorny branches that he had used to play Puck. He bowed down in a deliberate emulation of the crucified one with a crown of thorns, and then took his own life with his father's pistol. It was a desperate expression of his power to resist, even with his father's means. It was the ultimate perversion of "seizing the day." In the redemptive irony of the film, the suicide occurred while the other members of the Dead Poets Society were chanting the refrain from Vachel Lindsay's poem "General William Booth Enters Into Heaven": "Are you washed in the blood of the Lamb?"[23]

Restraint could have preserved the life of this promising young man. It might have provided time for gradual understanding and maturing, for Neil to start and complete his college education so that he would be in a position to sustain his independence from his father, even if the father remained tyrannical. But Neil's education had skipped over the poetry of restraint. As the headmaster discovered in taking over John Keating's classroom at the end of the film, the boys had studied the Romantics but not the Realists.[24] They had plumbed the depths of love, reveling in its fantasies, but had not been sobered by the poetry of self-control. The result, as foreseen by the Greek moralists, the Hebrew wisdom writers, and the author of 2 Timothy, was predictably tragic.

The same must be said with regard to our effort to reconceive Paul as the apostle to America. If power without love is destructive, then love without restraint is deadly. We all enjoy and need the inspired messages of love and faith, the thrilling power of Paul's egalitarian gospel. But if our interpretation is to be healthy, we also need the everyday sobriety of the Pauline sense of limits, the acknowledgment of ourselves as earthen vessels, and the recognition that our vision is always distorted by the tendency to suppress the truth. So the "Saint" Paul of the pastoral letters reflects a portion of his legitimate legacy in urging leaders to recognize that "God did not give us a spirit of timidity, but of power and love and self-restraint."

The Poet and the Interpreter

I would therefore like to invite you to consider handling these Pauline materials as if you belonged to a Dead Poets Society and more. This legacy includes the tradition of Lois and Eunice, of Paul and Timothy, of Luther and Barth, of Käsemann, Dodd, Dunn, and a host of others who now encompass the ecumenical world of biblical interpretation, past and present. To be true to this legacy requires that we move beyond the traditional parameters of interpretation, as each of them did in his or her time. Like the students of Keating's class at the end of the movie, we should find ourselves at times defying traditional limits to stand on the tops of our desks in rebellious tribute. The legacy of Paul constantly calls us into a commitment to the inspired poetry of the gospel— "the force" in a finally redemptive mode. It places us in the uncomfortable position of constantly being pulled this way and that by the gift of the spirit and the weight of ancestral traditions. It evokes an ongoing dialogue between the inspired movies of our time and the inspired texts of our religious traditions. It calls us to reignite whatever gifts we have received, and to modulate the power of the spirit with love and restraint, to guard against deadly loss. It warns us against the illusion of "a separate peace" and urges us to accept ourselves as "ordinary people." It exposes the yearning for vengeance that undercuts our idealistic zeal and it provides us with "the armor of light."

The poet to whom the committed Pauline interpreter should give final allegiance is Jesus, the carpenter's son who burst out of his parental home filled with the spirit of God, telling marvelous stories and creating poetic sayings to transform the world. For us, Christ is the profoundest of all poets, whose life, death, and resurrection opened the depths of truth for all later poets to explore. But he is more than a "dead poet" to us who believe. He is alive and in our midst, making himself known where two or three break bread in his name, opening their hearts to one another and sharing the "comfort of Christ" in a new creation. Although he remains as invisible as the "God of tender mercies," Christ joins us on the path of interpretation as we encounter the challenging stories of our culture, as we seek to derive wisdom from this encounter to meet the complex challenges of our time. He calls us to seize the day, to grasp the opportunity to reignite our gift and to reaffirm our place in a live poets society that will continue on and on, until history reaches its appointed end. "For God did not give us a spirit of timidity, but of power and love and self-restraint."

Notes

Quotations of dialogue from films discussed in this book are the author's transcriptions from the films, unless otherwise noted.

1. Pauline Theology Takes In the Movies

1. See the discussion of the strophic pattern in Gordon D. Fee, *The First Epistle to the Corinthians* (Grand Rapids: Wm. B. Eerdmans Publishing Co., 1987), 423.

2. Ibid., 424.

3. See Quentin J. Schultze et al., *Dancing in the Dark: Youth, Popular Culture and the Electronic Media* (Grand Rapids: Wm. B. Eerdmans Publishing Co., 1991), 76–110.

4. Ronald F. Hock, "The Workshop as a Social Setting for Paul's Missionary Preaching," *Catholic Biblical Quarterly* 41 (1979), 438–450; see also Hock's *The Social Context of Paul's Ministry: Tentmaking and Apostleship* (Philadelphia: Fortress Press, 1980).

5. See *Christian Tolerance: Paul's Message to the Modern Church* (Philadelphia: Westminster Press, 1982); *Romans*, Teacher Book and Student Book for the "Genesis to Revelation Adult Bible Series," vol. 20 (Nashville: Graded Press of the United Methodist Publishing House, 1986); *Romans,* in the "Cokesbury Basic Bible Commentary" series (Nashville: United Methodist Publishing House, 1988).

6. The tentative title is *Paul, the Apostle to America* (Louisville, Ky.: Westminster/John Knox Press, forthcoming).

7. See the studies of biblical spectaculars by Ivan Butler, *Religion in the Cinema* (New York: A. S. Barnes & Co., 1969), 9–32, and Gerald E. Forshey, "American Religious and Biblical Spectacular Films, 1932–1975," Ph.D. dissertation, University of Chicago, 1978, which was revised as *American Religious and Biblical Spectaculars* (Westport, Conn.: Praeger, 1992). The study of Christ and Christ figures by Peter Malone, *Movie Christs and Antichrists* (New York: Crossroad, 1990), is not very relevant for the Pauline letters, while James M. Wall, *Church and Cinema: A Way of Viewing Film* (Grand Rapids: Wm. B. Eerdmans Publishing Co., 1971), deals with "life-values" rather than biblical materials.

8. See for example the pioneering work of Neil P. Hurley, who proposes an "alliance of cinema and theology" in *Theology Through Film* (New York: Harper & Row, 1970) and deals with the biblical model of liberation from bondage in *The Reel Revolution: A Film Primer on Liberation* (Maryknoll, N.Y.: Orbis Books, 1978).

9. John R. May and Michael S. Bird, eds., *Religion in Film* (Knoxville: University of Tennessee Press, 1982), ix. See also *Image and Likeness: Religious Visions in American Film Classics,* ed. John R. May (New York: Paulist Press, 1992).

10. Richard A. Blake, S.J., *Screening America: Reflections on Five Classic Films* (New York: Paulist Press, 1991).

11. Ibid., 289.

12. See Robert S. Corrington, *The Community of Interpreters: On the Hermeneutics of Nature and the Bible in the American Philosophical Tradition* (Macon, Ga.: Mercer University Press, 1987).

2. *Star Wars* and "the Force" of Paul's Gospel

1. *Star Wars* was a Twentieth Century-Fox production of 1977 by "Lucasfilm Limited Production." The videotape of the film is distributed by CBS/Fox Video. An additional video concerning the production of the film is titled *The Making of Star Wars: As Told by C3PO and R2D2*, produced and distributed by CBS/FOX Video, 1987. A comic book version of *Star Wars* was published by Marvel Comics, New York, 1978.

2. George Lucas, *Star Wars: From the Adventures of Luke Skywalker* (New York: Ballantine Books, 1976), 207.

3. Ibid.,1.

4. Richard Slotkin, *Regeneration Through Violence: The Mythology of the American Frontier, 1600–1860* (Middletown, Conn.: Wesleyan University Press, 1973).

5. Robert E. A. Lee overlooks these details in his contention that "*Star Wars* has an undergirding religious premise that is theologically simplistic but nonetheless impressively reverent and sincerely introduced. Alec Guinness calls his god 'the Force' and inspires young Luke also to become a disciple of and a believer in 'the Force.' It is a combination of the mysticism of ESP and the New Testament doctrine of the Holy Spirit." *The Lutheran* (July 13, 1977), 30.

6. Cited by Carl Cohen, ed., *Communism, Fascism and Democracy: The Theoretical Foundations* (New York: Random House, 1972), 346.

7. Lucas, *Star Wars*, 120.

8. Cohen, *Communism, Fascism and Democracy*, 332.

9. William Siska, "A Breath of Fresh Fantasy," *The Christian Century* 94 (July 20–27, 1977), 667.

10. See, for example, Jouette M. Bassler, *Divine Impartiality: Paul and a Theological Axiom*, SBL Dissertation Series 59 (Chico, Calif.: Scholars Press, 1982), 121–170.

11. Ernst Käsemann, *Commentary on Romans*, trans. G. W. Bromiley (Grand Rapids: Wm. B. Eerdmans Publishing Co., 1980), 29.

12. James D. G. Dunn, *Romans 1–8* (Dallas: Word Books, 1988), 48.

13. Lucas, *Star Wars*, 79–80.

14. In his path-breaking study *Glaube als Teilhabe. Historische und semantische Grundlagen der paulinischen Theologie und Ekklesiologie des Glaubens* (Tübingen: J. C. B. Mohr [Paul Siebeck], 1987), Axel von Dobbeler shows that faith involves participation in Christian communities, involving solidarity between cultural groups.

15. Lucas, *Star Wars*, 121.

16. Ibid., 77; elision in the original.

17. Cohen, *Communism, Fascism and Democracy*, 314.

18. Ibid., 334.

3. *Amadeus:* Sin, Salvation, and Salieri

1. This rhetorical analysis is adapted from Leander Keck, "The Function of Rom. 3:10–18," pp. 142–146 in *God's Christ and His People: Studies in Honour of Nils Alstrup Dahl*, ed. J. Jervell and W. A. Meeks (Oslo: Universitetsforlaget, 1977).

2. The film was directed by Milos Forman and produced by Saul Zaentz; an Orion Pictures Release, 1984. The videotape is available through HBO/Cannon Video, 1984. The original play is by Peter Schaffer, *Peter Schaffer's Amadeus* (New York: Harper & Row, 1981; New American Library, 1984).

3. Alan Rich protests the moral stereotyping in the film as anachronistic, since Mozart's behavior would not have elicited "much horror in the time of *Tom Jones* or Goetz von Berlichingen." See "Amadeus—A Fabric of Falsehoods," *Ovation* 5, Number 11 (1984), 40.

4. Käsemann, *Romans*, 86; C. E. B. Cranfield, *A Critical and Exegetical Commentary on the Epistle to the Romans* (Edinburgh: T. & T. Clark, 1975), 191: "Paul thinks of sin as a power which has got control of man, and there is a marked tendency to personification in his references to it." For a critique of this view, see Günter Röhser, *Metaphorik und Personifikation der Sünde. Antike Sündenvorstellungen und paulinischen Hamartia* (Tübingen: J. C. B. Mohr [Paul Siebeck], 1987).

5. Karl Barth, *The Epistle to the Romans*, trans. E. C. Hoskyns (Oxford: Oxford University Press, 1933), 85.

6. C. K. Barrett, *The Epistle to the Romans* (New York: Harper & Row, 1957), 34.

7. Cranfield, *Romans*, 112.

8. Barrett, *Romans*, 37.

9. Vincent Canby, in "The Voice of God," *New York Times* (September 19, 1984), notes some of the differences between the original play and the movie, suggesting that the latter "may be even more humane than the play."

10. This and all subsequent quotations are my transcriptions of dialogue from the film rather than from the play by Peter Schaffer, unless otherwise noted.

11. Samuel Terrien, *"Amadeus* Revisited," *Theology Today* 42 (1986), 437.

12. Ibid., 437, cited from Schaffer, *Peter Schaffer's Amadeus,* 182.

13. Terrien, *"Amadeus* Revisited," 439–440.

14. Karl Barth, *Wolfgang Amadeus Mozart,* trans. C. K. Pott; foreword by J. Updike (Grand Rapids: Wm. B. Eerdmans Publishing Co., 1986), 16, 33–34.

15. Ibid., 53.

16. This is overlooked by Terrien in *"Amadeus* Revisited," 440–442.

17. That the catena of quotations in Rom. 3:10–18 was created by an early Christian scholar and quoted by Paul has been argued by Otto Michel in *Der Brief an die Römer* (Göttingen: Vandenhoeck & Ruprecht, 1966), 143, and Keck in "Function of Rom. 3:10–18," 146–147. The Pauline authorship of the catena is emphasized in the most recent investigation by Dietrich-Alex Koch, *Die Schrift als Zeuge des Evangeliums. Untersuchungen zur Verwendung und zum Verständnis der Schrift bei Paulus* (Tübingen: J. C. B. Mohr [Paul Siebeck], 1986), 179–184.

18. See also Terrien, *"Amadeus* Revisited," 438: "a name which suggests 'the gift of God, the love of God, the one whom God loves.'"

19. Ibid., 441.

20. Terrien quotes an editor of *The Christian Century* as charging that Shaffer's play "finally insinuates a cynical view of life which is far worse than a courageously maintained nihilism." Ibid., 435.

21. Charles Wesley, "O for a Thousand Tongues to Sing," *The United Methodist Hymnal: Book of United Methodist Worship* (Nashville: Methodist Publishing House, 1989), 57, verse 4.

4. *A Separate Peace* with Adam's Fall

1. I am following Stanley E. Porter, who has made a compelling text-critical case for the subjunctive, requiring the translation "let us have peace," in "The Argument of Romans 5: Can a Rhetorical Question Make a Difference?" *Journal of Biblical Literature* 110 (1991), 662–665.

2. Richard W. Lewis, *American Adam* (Chicago: University of Chicago Press, 1955).

3. Cited by Hans Kohn, *American Nationalism: An Interpretive Essay* (New York: Macmillan Publishing Co., 1957), 13.

4. John Knowles, *A Separate Peace* (New York: Macmillan Publishing Co., 1959; citations from the Bantam edition (New York: Bantam Books, 1966).

5. *A Separate Peace* was produced by Robert A. Goldston, directed by Larry Peerce, and distributed by Paramount Pictures in 1972. The video was distributed by Paramount in 1989.

6. Knowles, *Separate Peace*, 41.

7. Vincent Canby describes Phineas as a "natural man . . . the kind of innocent favored in romantic literature, incapable of viciousness and simply puzzled when he recognizes it in others." *New York Times* (September 28, 1972).

8. Knowles, *Separate Peace*, 194–195.

9. Ibid., 27.

10. Ibid., 17.

11. See Cranfield, *Romans*, 269–270. for a sketch of the issues and an extensive bibliography on the role of Adam's fall in Pauline thought. See especially Morna D. Hooker, "Adam in Romans i," *New Testament Studies* 6 (1959–60), 297–306, and A. J. M. Wedderburn, "The Theological Structure of Romans 5.12," *New Testament Studies* 19 (1972–73), 339-354.

12. See Claus Westermann, *Genesis* (Neukirchen-Vluyn: Neukirchener Verlag, 1966), 337; Gerhard von Rad, *Genesis: A Commentary*, trans. J. H. Marks (London: SCM Press, 1961).

13. See Paul J. Achtemeier, *Romans* (Atlanta: John Knox Press, 1983), 38–39.

14. Käsemann, *Romans*, 148. See also Daniel Patte, *Paul's Faith and the Power of the Gospel: A Structural Introduction to the Pauline Letters* (Philadelphia: Fortress Press, 1983), 252: "what Paul says about evil in its various manifestations reveals two apparently contradictory kinds of affirmations. On the one hand, Paul emphasizes that human beings are responsible for evil. . . . On the other hand, humans are under the power of evil."

15. Paul D. Zimmerman, "Beneath the Levis," *Newsweek* 80 (October 16, 1972), 106.

16. The narration by Gene at the beginning of the film, when he returns to Devon after the war, includes the line: "Now that I was back after all these years, I was surprised to see how peaceful it looked."

17. Knowles, *Separate Peace*, 37: "There were few relationships among us at Devon not based on rivalry."

18. Ibid., 3.

19. Ibid., 193–194.

20. Ibid., 47.

21. Ibid., 46.

22. In this and some material cited below without notes, I have transcribed dialogue from the videotape of the film.

23. Cf. Roland Bartel, "Brief Comments on Other Works of Fiction with Biblical Allusions," in *Biblical Images in Literature,* ed. R. Bartel, J. S. Ackerman, and T. S. Warshaw, (Nashville: Abingdon Press, 1975), 186–187.

24. See Cranfield, *Romans,* 278–281.

25. Knowles, *Separate Peace,* 195.

26. See the discussion of this passage in Cranfield, *Romans,* 256–257.

27. C. H. Dodd, *The Epistle of Paul to the Romans* (London: Hodder & Stoughton, 1932), 72–73, refers to "the state of hostility between Him and us in which our sin had placed us."

28. See the exposition in Ralph P. Martin, *Reconciliation: A Study of Paul's Theology* (Atlanta: John Knox Press, 1981), 135–152.

29. William Sampson, "Liberty Weekend Left Out Blacks," *Chicago Sun-Times* (July 8, 1986), 31.

30. "Liberty Celebration," *World Press Review* (August 1986), 17.

5. The Mysterious God of *Tender Mercies*

1. *Tender Mercies* was directed by Bruce Beresford and produced by Philip S. Hobel. It was released by Universal Pictures in 1983. The screenplay by Horton Foote received an Academy Award. The videotape is available from HBO Video, 1988. The play by Horton Foote was published in *To Kill a Mockingbird, Tender Mercies, and the Trip to Bountiful: Three Screenplays* (New York: Grove Weidenfeld, 1989).

2. John Van Seters suggests that these two statements were linked in an early form of the Abraham story; see *Abraham in History and Tradition* (New Haven, Conn.: Yale University Press, 1975), 224.

3. For a discussion of the birth of Isaac story in the context

of other ancient Near Eastern stories of divine promise of an heir for an elderly couple, see Van Seter, *Abraham*, 202–208.

4. Apocalypse of Baruch 57:2, cited by Dodd in *Romans*, 68.

5. Barrett, *Romans*, 95–96. See also the commentaries by Sanday-Headlam and Lagrange, and see especially Cranfield, *Romans*, 242.

6. Käsemann, *Romans*, 121.

7. Most commentators stress that the "all" in v. 16 includes Jewish and Gentile Christians; for instance Dodd (*Romans*, 70) speaks of the "universality of the Christian religion" at this point. But Paul seems explicitly to go beyond such parameters to include persons of Jewish faith as well by the formulation "not only to those of the law" in Rom. 4:16.

8. Richard A. Blake, "Texas Agape," *America* (April 23, 1983), 322.

9. Ibid., 322.

10. Samuel G. Freedman, "From the Heart of Texas," *New York Times Magazine* (February 9, 1986), 50.

11. Janet Maslin aptly observes: "Like its laconic characters, the film itself seems to have more on its mind than it can manage to say." "Tale of Two Wives," *New York Times* (March 4, 1983).

12. Pauline Kael, "The Current Cinema," *New Yorker* (May 16, 1983), 120.

13. See the discussion in Michel, *Römer*, 171, and Otfried Hofius, "Eine altjüdische Parallele zu Röm 4.17b," *New Testament Studies* 18 (1971–72), 93–94.

14. Käsemann, *Romans*, 123.

15. This phrase appears to be a direct quotation of the second benediction in the traditional Eighteen Benediction prayer of rabbinic Judaism, which in this context would pick up the theme of Abraham's aged body being "as good as dead" (Rom. 4:19). But the lifting up of this theme expresses also the central motif of Paul's Christian faith; it is as if the Abraham story were being viewed through the lens of Jesus' resurrection. See Cranfield, *Romans*, 244, and Ulrich Wilckens, *Der Brief an die Römer* (Zurich: Benzinger, 1978), 1: 274.

16. See Dunn, *Romans*, 237: "the individual or nation is dependent on the unconditional grace of God as much for

covenant life as for created life. It was this total dependence on God for very existence itself which man forgot, his rejection of that dependence which lies at the root of his malaise (1:18–28)."

17. Colin L. Westerbeck, Jr., "Unsung Heroes: Robert Duvall in 'Tender Mercies,'" *Commonweal* 118 (April 8, 1983), 210.

18. Blake, "Texas Agape," 322.

19. Robert Hatch, "Tender Mercies . . . ," *The Nation* 236 (April 30, 1983), 554.

20. Philip A. Siddons in *Christianity Today* notes, however, that the theological content of this God is "humanistic" and syncretistic. "'Oh, God!' Oh, Carl Reiner!" vol. 22 (Dec. 30, 1977), 23–24.

21. For an exposition of this theme, see Samuel L. Terrien, *The Elusive Presence: Toward a New Biblical Theology* (San Francisco: Harper & Row, 1978).

6. Righteous Gentiles in *Grand Canyon*

1. Käsemann, in *Romans*, 244, refers to the "careful rhetorical construction" of the clauses in this sentence, "which are linked in a mounting chain."

2. The film *Grand Canyon* was directed and produced by Lawrence Kasdan and distributed by Twentieth Century-Fox in 1991. The screenplay was written by Lawrence and Meg Kasdan. The video is available from Letterboxed editions, Waltham, Mass.: Sight & Sound, 1991.

3. David Ansen, "Peter Pan, Get Lost," *Newsweek* 118 (December 30, 1991), 57.

4. Klyne R. Snodgrass, "Justification by Grace—To the Doers: An Analysis of the Place of Romans 2 in the Theology of Paul," *New Testament Studies* 32 (1986), 72–93.

5. Ibid., 80.

6. Ibid., 84.

7. See Dunn, *Romans*, 102.

8. Snodgrass, "Justification," 79; see also 83.

9. Ibid., 82.

10. See Robert Jewett, "Paul, Phoebe, and the Spanish Mission," in *The Social World of Formative Christianity and Judaism: Essays in Tribute to Howard Clark Kee,* ed. Peder Borgen et al. (Philadelphia: Fortress Press, 1988), 144–164.

11. Stanley Kauffmann, "Troubled People," *The New Republic* 206 (January 20, 1992), 28.

12. Dunn, *Romans*, 107.

13. See John Gregory Dunne, "Law and Disorder in Los Angeles," *New York Review of Books* 38 (October 10, 1991), 23.

14. See the excerpts from Daryl F. Gates's book, *Chief: My Life in the LAPD* (New York: Bantam Books, 1992) in *Newsweek* (May 11, 1992, 39) which identifies the first task of law enforcement as "identify the enemy." Ira Socol observes that "the L. A. bosses compared their city to Vietnam" and that the Gates strategy in effect was to declare "war" on their neighbors ("Trained to Do Our Dirty Work for Us," *New York Times* [May 2, 1992]).

15. Käsemann, *Romans*, 243; see also Cranfield, *Romans*, 429.

16. Dunn, *Romans*, 481.

17. Ansen, "Peter Pan, Get Lost," 57.

7. *Tootsie* and the Comfort of Christ

1. *Tootsie* was produced in 1982 by Columbia Pictures. The video is distributed by RCA/Columbia Pictures Home Video, 1983–91.

2. Victor Paul Furnish, *II Corinthians: Translated with Introduction, Notes, and Commentary* (Garden City, N.Y.: Doubleday & Co., 1984), 52.

3. Dieter Georgi, *The Opponents of Paul in Second Corinthians* (Philadelphia: Fortress Press, 1986), 229–314.

4. Furnish, *II Corinthians*, 130, citing a phrase by Rudolf Bultmann.

5. Ibid., 159.

6. Vincent Canby, "When a Movie Doesn't Have to Pass the Plausibility Test," *New York Times* (January 2, 1983).

7. See Ronald F. Hock, *The Social Context of Paul's Ministry: Tentmaking and Apostleship* (Philadelphia: Fortress Press, 1980).

8. Furnish concludes that the most likely suggestion is that the "affliction in Asia" was an Ephesian imprisonment not mentioned in the book of Acts; *II Corinthians*, 122–123.

9. Translation by Furnish, in *II Corinthians*, 168; he repudiates Barrett's suggestion that Paul was anxious about the risk Titus was running from robbery since he was collecting money

for the Jerusalem Offering, concluding instead that the anxiety was due to Paul's "concern" about the congregation with whom his relationships had been strained; 171.

10. Declan Kiberd, *Men and Feminism in Modern Literature* (New York: St. Martin's Press, 1985), 33.

11. It is also interesting in this regard that Dustin Hoffman gave a number of interviews "about how playing Dorothy has changed his life . . . ," to the irritation of his reviewers; see John Simon, "New Woman, Old Newman," *National Review* (February 4, 1983), 131–132.

12. Cf. Furnish, *II Corinthians*, 118–121.

13. Richard A. Blake, "Role Models," *America* 148 (January 29, 1983), 74.

14. Cf. Robert Jewett, *Paul's Anthropological Terms: A Study of Their Use in Conflict Settings* (Leiden: E. J. Brill, 1971), 259–263.

15. Henri J. M. Nouwen, *The Wounded Healer: Ministry in Contemporary Society* (Garden City, N.Y.: Doubleday & Co., 1979), 88.

8. Earthen Vessels and *Ordinary People*

1. For a discussion of the rhetorical structure of this passage see John T. Fitzgerald, *Cracks in an Earthen Vessel: An Examination of the Catalogues of Hardships in the Corinthian Correspondence* (Atlanta: Scholars Press, 1988), 172.

2. Judith Guest, *Ordinary People* (New York: Ballantine Books, 1977).

3. *Ordinary People* was directed by Robert Redford and produced by Ronald L. Schwary. It was released by Paramount Pictures in 1980. The video is available from Paramount Home Video, 1980.

4. See John Passmore, *The Perfectibility of Man* (London: Gerald Duckworth & Co., 1970).

5. Richard Fenn, *The Dream of the Perfect Act: An Inquiry Into the Fate of Religion in a Secular World* (New York/London: Tavistock, 1987), viii.

6. Robert Jewett and John Shelton Lawrence, *The American Monomyth*, 2d ed. (Lanham, Md.: University Press of America, 1988).

7. Thomas C. Oden and Leicester R. Longden, *The Wesleyan Theological Heritage: Essays of Albert C. Outler* (Grand Rapids: Zondervan Publishing House, 1991), 121–122; see also 51: "Wesley never qualified his claim that 'perfection' was his most nearly distinctive doctrine. But he was lamentably unsuccessful in explaining it. . . . I think that I now can show that at least a good deal of the cross talk came from the fact that Wesley's critics were denying the Latin tradition of *perfectus est* (made perfect, i.e. static or completed perfection) while Wesley was affirming a somewhat impressionistic version of the Eastern tradition of *teleiosis* (becoming perfect)."

8. Ralph Martin, *2 Corinthians* (Waco, Tex.: Word, 1986), 85; Furnish, *II Corinthians*, 253, 278.

9. C. K. Barrett, in *A Commentary on the Second Epistle to the Corinthians* (New York: Harper & Row, 1973), 137–138, develops the contrast between the common pot and "infinitely valuable treasure of the Gospel."

10. Furnish, *II Corinthians*, 278: "Pottery vessels, unlike those made of glass or precious metal, have value only while they are whole and intact. . . . They are cheap but fragile, and therefore they are of no enduring value. That means, also, that they are expendable."

11. The Old Testament cultic regulations demanded the smashing of polluted earthenware (Lev. 11:33 and 15:12).

12. Barrett, *Second Epistle to the Corinthians*, 138.

13. Fitzgerald, *Cracks in an Earthen Vessel*, 167–168.

14. Richard A. Blake develops a similar metaphor, that the Jarretts are "like a Belleek tea service. They . . . are fragile, and once removed from the shelf, they know that they risk shattering those delicate surfaces." "Surfaces," *America* 143 (October 18, 1980), 231.

15. See especially Marion Woodman, *Addiction to Perfection: The Still Unravished Bride, A Psychological Study*, Studies in Jungian Psychology by Jungian Analysts 12 (Toronto: Inner City, 1982), 10.

16. Pauline Kael, "The Current Cinema," *New Yorker* 56 (October 13, 1980), 180.

17. Furnish, in *II Corinthians*, 254, suggests the translation "under pressure, but not crushed."

18. I concur with Furnish (*II Corinthians*, 255) that the term

diôkein should be translated as "persecute" rather than merely "pursue," as in a race.

19. Woodman, *Addiction to Perfection*, 52; see also 188: "To strive for perfection is to kill love because perfection does not recognize humanity."

20. Warren Farrell, *Why Men Are the Way They Are: The Male-Female Dynamic* (New York: McGraw-Hill Book Co., 1986), 97, 113.

21. See Furnish, *II Corinthians*, 254.

22. Kael, "The Current Cinema," (October 13, 1980), 189.

23. Guest, *Ordinary People*, 9.

24. Ibid., 217.

25. Ibid., 235.

26. Ibid., 163.

27. Ibid., 83–84.

28. Ibid., 149, 151, 218.

29. See Martin, *2 Corinthians*, 87; Furnish, in *II Corinthians*, 255, argues that the boxing metaphor was not originally intended by Paul because of the overly strong term used in the second half of the expression, "struck down, but not *destroyed*."

30. Herbert Hendin, *Suicide in America* (New York: W. W. Norton & Co., 1982), 30–36.

31. Guest, *Ordinary People*, 107.

32. See Gerald E. Forshey, "Struggling Toward Autonomy," *The Christian Century* 97 (November 26, 1980), 1170.

33. William Stephens Taylor, "Perfectionism in Psychology and in Theology," *Canadian Journal of Theology* 5 (1959), 170–179.

34. Guest, *Ordinary People*, 208.

35. Ibid., 112; also 158, 233.

36. Ibid., 127.

37. See Furnish, *II Corinthians*, 255.

38. Guest, *Ordinary People*, 185.

39. Ibid., 223.

40. Ibid., 241.

41. See Kael, "Current Cinema" (October 13, 1980), 190.

42. Guest, *Ordinary People*, 245.

43. Fitzgerald, *Cracks in an Earthen Vessel*, 170.

44. See the extensive discussion of this crucial verse in Fitzgerald, *Cracks in an Earthen Vessel*, 176–180.

45. See Robert Jewett, *A Chronology of Paul's Life* (Philadelphia: Fortress Press, 1979), 45.

9. *Empire of the Sun* and the Death of Innocence

1. *Empire of the Sun* was directed and produced by Steven Spielberg, with a screenplay by Tom Stoppard, and released by Warner Brothers in 1987. The video is available from Warner Home Video, 1987.

2. Helen North, *Sophrosyne: Self-Knowledge and Self-Restraint in Greek Literature,* Cornell Studies in Classical Philology 35 (Ithaca, N.Y.: Cornell University Press, 1966), ix.

3. *Time* (March 14, 1988).

4. Otto Friedrich, "Up, Up and Awaaay!!!" *Time* (March 14, 1988), 68.

5. Ibid., 74.

6. Vincent Canby, "Evoking Childhood Isn't Kid Stuff," *New York Times* (February 7, 1988).

7. Janet Maslin refers to "Jim's near-religious experiences with the fighter planes he sees as halfway divine." *New York Times* (December 9, 1987).

8. North, *Sophrosyne,* 1–31.

9. Ibid., 22–25.

10. Ibid., 12.

11. Ibid., 14.

12. Myra Forsberg, "Spielberg at 40: The Man and the Child," *New York Times* (January 10, 1988).

13. Ibid.

14. For an elaboration of this idea, see Robert Jewett, *Christian Tolerance,* 43–67.

15. Friedrich, "Up, Up and Awaaay!!!" 70.

16. Ibid.

17. Ibid.

18. Robert Jewett and John Shelton Lawrence, *The American Monomyth,* 2d ed. (Lanham, Md.: University Press of America, 1988).

19. J. G. Ballard, *Empire of the Sun* (New York: Washington Square, 1984), 138, 144.

20. Ibid., 198–199. See also 216.

21. Ibid., 120: "At home, if he did anything wrong, the consequences seemed to overlay everything for days. With Basie they vanished instantly. For the first time in his life Jim felt free to do what he wanted. All sorts of wayward ideas moved through his mind, fueled by hunger and the excitement of stealing from the old prisoners."

22. Ibid., 183.

23. Mythic alchemy is visible in the accentuation of the global redemption scheme in the Stoppard/Spielberg version of Jim's statement. The Ballard novel has Jim say "I can bring him back, I can bring him back, I can bring them all back, I can bring him back."

24. Ballard, *Empire*, 364–365.

25. Ibid., 375.

10. The Disguise of Vengeance in *Pale Rider*

1. See the rhetorical analysis of this material in Walter T. Wilson, *Love Without Pretense: Romans 12:9–21 and Hellenistic-Jewish Wisdom Literature* (Tübingen: J. C. B. Mohr [Paul Siebeck], 1991), 132–136.

2. *Pale Rider* was directed and produced by Clint Eastwood and released by Warner Brothers in 1985. The video is available from Warner Home Video, 1985. The adaptation of the screenplay is by Alan Dean Foster: *Pale Rider: A Novelization* (New York: Warner Books, 1985; London: Arrow, 1985; Leicester: Linford, 1987).

3. This material about *The Virginian* is adapted from Jewett and Lawrence, *American Monomyth*, 180–185.

4. See Tom Shales, "Reign of TV Terror Floods Viewers in Vigilantism," *Chicago Tribune* (January 17, 1986).

5. Foster, *Pale Rider*, 13–14.

6. Ibid., 53.

7. Vincent Canby, "Vengeance Is His," *New York Times* (June 28, 1985).

8. Stephen Chapman, "Who Is the Pale Rider?" *Chicago Tribune* (July 7, 1985).

9. Foster, *Pale Rider*, 129.

10. Ibid., 113.

11. John M. Kraps reports this detail in "The Gospel

According to Eastwood," *The Christian Century* 102 (August 14, 1985), 740.

12. Foster, *Pale Rider*, 215.

13. Ibid., 45.

14. Ibid., 170.

15. I am not inclined to follow Vincent Canby's suggestion in "Vengeance Is His" that "resurrection also is the key to 'Pale Rider.'" I am more inclined to agree that "just who this fellow was in his previous incarnation is left so vague you have a right to suspect that he might have been Him."

16. Foster, *Pale Rider*, 190.

17. See Will Wright's discussion of the "vengeance variation" in *Six-Guns and Society: A Structural Study of the Western* (Berkeley, Calif.: University of California Press, 1975), 59–74.

18. Jacob M. Braude, *Lifetime Speaker's Encyclopedia* (Englewood Cliffs, N.J.: Prentice-Hall, 1962), II: 700, quoting Thomas Wilson.

19. William Klassen, "Coals of Fire: Sign of Repentance or Revenge," *New Testament Studies* 9 (1962–63), 337–350.

20. Robert Jewett and John Shelton Lawrence, "The Fantasy Factor in Civil Religion: Assassinations and Mass Murders in the Media Age," presented at the April 2–3 meeting of the American Academy of Religion at Rockford, Ill.; subsequently revised and published in *explor* 7 (1982). The article has been reprinted in *Sunstone* 7 (September–October, 1983), 28–33, and *Mission Journal* 17.2 (1983), 3–7, 17.

21. Burton F. Stevenson, *The Home Book of Quotations: Classical and Modern* (New York: Dodd, Mead & Co., 1967), 1711.

11. Works of Darkness in *Red Dawn*

1. Peter Goldman et al., "Rocky and Rambo," *Newsweek* (December 23, 1985), 58.

2. Ibid., 62; see also Michael Musto, "Bloody Awful," *Saturday Review* (July–August 1985), 82: "the really unfortunate thing about Rambo is that it happens to be slick, expertly made, well filmed, and calculated to strike just the right chords in a macho audience's nervous system."

3. Siegfried Kracauer, *From Caligari to Hitler: A Psychological History of the German Film* (Princeton, N.J.: Princeton University Press, 1947).

4. *Red Dawn* was directed by John Milius, with a screenplay by Kevin Reynolds and John Milius, and produced by Buzz Feitshans and Barry Beckerman. It was released by MGM/UA Entertainment Company in 1984. The videotape is available from MGM/UA Home Video, 1985.

5. Cranfield, *Romans*, 687.

6. Walter Bauer, William F. Arndt, F. Wilbur Gingrich, and Frederick W. Danker, *A Greek-English Lexicon of the New Testament and Other Early Christian Literature* (Chicago: University of Chicago Press, 1979), 461.

7. David Morrell, *Rambo: First Blood Part II*, from the screenplay by Sylvester Stallone and James Cameron (New York: Harcourt Brace Jovanovich, Jove Books, 1985), 69.

8. Jewett and Lawrence, *American Monomyth*.

9. Bruce J. Malina, *The New Testament World: Insights from Cultural Anthropology* (Atlanta: John Knox Press, 1981), 53–70.

10. Cited from a letter to the editor of *New York Magazine* in the summer of 1985, quoted by J. Hoberman, "The Fascist Guns," *American Film* (March, 1986), 42.

11. Ibid., 48.

12. J. W. Scott, "The Politics of Virility: Review of *French Fascism: The First Wave 1924–1933* by Robert Soucy," *New York Times Book Review* (April 20, 1986), 21.

13. See Janet Maslin, "Hey, Don't Forget the Audience," *New York Times* (August 19, 1984). But in "Summer Sets the Crackpot Bubbling," *New York Times* (September 2, 1984), Maslin acknowledges the "dismaying popularity of Mr. Milius's film."

14. Harry Cheney, "Cinema: *Red Dawn*," *Christianity Today* 28 (October 19, 1984), 60.

15. See Käsemann, *Romans*, 363.

16. See Jewett, *Anthropological Terms*, 165.

17. Jonathan Broder, "Terrorists' Europe Even Scares Rambo," *Chicago Tribune* (May 8, 1986).

18. *Chicago Tribune* (June 6, 1986).

12. "Saint" Paul and *Dead Poets Society*

1. For the assessment of the linguistic evidence of post-Pauline authorship, see A. Q. Morton and James McLeman, *Paul, the Man and the Myth: A Study in the Authorship of Greek*

Prose (New York: Harper & Row, 1966); P. N. Harrison, *Paulines and Pastorals* (London: Villiers, 1964); Kenneth J. Neumann, *The Authenticity of the Pauline Letters in the Light of Stylostatistical Analysis* (Atlanta: Scholars Press, 1990), esp. 217–218. The case against Pauline authorship on a variety of grounds is set forth in Martin Dibelius and Hans Conzelmann, *The Pastoral Epistles: A Commentary on the Pastoral Epistles*, trans. P. Buttolph and A. Yarbro, ed. H. Koester (Philadelphia: Fortress Press, 1972), and Arland J. Hultgren, *I–II Timothy, Titus* (Minneapolis: Augsburg, 1984), 12–30. A recent defense of Pauline authorship, using a secretary hypothesis, is set forth by Michael Prior in *Paul the Letter-Writer and the Second Letter to Timothy* (Sheffield: Sheffield Academic Press, 1989).

2. *Dead Poets Society* was produced by Steven Haft and others for Touchstone Pictures in association with Silver Screen Partners IV and released by Buena Vista in 1989. It was directed by Peter Weir. The video is distributed by Touchstone Home Video, 1990. The script of the Academy Award–winning screenplay is published by Tom Schulman: *The Dead Poets Society* (Hollywood: Script City, 1988; revised third draft), and a novelistic version of the film was written by N. H. Kleinbaum: *Dead Poets Society* (New York: Bantam Books, 1989).

3. Quoted from Kleinbaum, *Dead Poets Society*, 2.

4. Ibid., 123.

5. See Hultgren, *I–II Timothy, Titus*, 109.

6. Thomas C. Oden, *First and Second Timothy and Titus* (Louisville: Westminster/John Knox Press, 1989), 28.

7. See Hultgren, *I–II Timothy, Titus*, 109.

8. See Winsome Munro, *Authority in Peter and Paul: The Identification of a Pastoral Stratum in the Pauline Corpus and I Peter*, Society for New Testament Studies Monograph Series 45 (Cambridge: Cambridge University Press, 1983), 101–103; Elisabeth Schüssler Fiorenza, *In Memory of Her: A Feminist Theological Reconstruction of Christian Origins* (New York: Crossroad, 1984), 288–291.

9. See Oden's reflections on "the maternal line and the absent father" in *First and Second Timothy and Titus*, 29–30.

10. Kleinbaum, *Dead Poets Society*, 2.

11. Ibid., 109.

12. See Dennis Ronald MacDonald, *The Legend and the*

Apostle: The Battle for Paul in Story and Canon (Philadelphia: Westminster Press, 1983), 40–53.

13. See Hultgren, *I–II Timothy, Titus*, 46–48.

14. Caryn James writes that the film "is harmed just as much by its villains—the stereotypical stern headmaster, the prissy textbook introduction to poetry that Keating makes his students tear out of their books, the student's father who exhibits Dickensian meanness. Nonconformity means nothing because conformity is made of straw men." *New York Times* (June 11, 1989).

15. See Hultgren, *I–II Timothy, Titus*, 110–111.

16. Cited directly from my transcription of dialogue from the film.

17. Kleinbaum, *Dead Poets Society*, 4.

18. Ibid., 4.

19. Ibid., 5.

20. Neil Perry defines excellence for Dean Nolan as follows: "Excellence is the result of hard work. . . . Excellence is the key to all success, in school and everywhere." Ibid., 5.

21. Ibid., 87.

22. Ibid., 82.

23. Ibid., 149–150.

24. Ibid., 163.

Index of Scripture

Index of Subjects and Names